THE PRICE OF PEACE

EMERGENCY ECONOMIC INTERVENTION AND U.S. FOREIGN POLICY

DAVID J. ROTHKOPF

CARNEGIE ENDOWMENT FOR INTERNATIONAL PEACE

**The Price of Peace: Emergency Economic Intervention
and U.S. Foreign Policy**
may be ordered ($10.95) from Carnegie Endowment's distributor:
The Brookings Institution Press
Department 029, Washington, D.C. 20042-0029, USA
Tel: 1-800-275-1447 or 202-797-6258
Fax: 202-797-6004, E-mail: bibooks@brook.edu

Cover photos (top to bottom): © *Christopher Morris/Black Star/PNI;
Andrew Lichtenstein/Impact Visuals/PNI; Peter Turnley/Black Star/PNI.
Design by Paddy McLaughlin Concepts & Design.
Printed by Automated Graphic Systems.*

Library of Congress Cataloging-in-Publication Data

Rothkopf, David J. (David Jochanan), 1955-
       The price of peace: emergency economic intervention and U.S. foreign
policy / David J. Rothkopf.
       p. cm.
       Includes bibliographical references.
       ISBN 0-87003-150-3 (pbk.)
       1. Economic assistance, American—Political aspects. 2. Economic
assistance, American—Haiti. 3. Economic assistance, American—Midle
East. 4. Economic assistance, American—Bosnia and Hercegovina.
5. United States—Foreign relations—1989-   I. Title.
HC60.R685 1998   98-17009
327.1'11—dc21   CIP

CONTENTS

ACKNOWLEDGMENTS

When I proposed the idea for this book in early 1996, Morton I. Abramowitz, then President of the Carnegie Endowment for International Peace, embraced the project. Throughout, Mort has been an unfailingly wise advisor and a warm, witty, and good friend. His successor, Jessica Tuchman Mathews, also offered a great deal in the way of much valued support and advice. In addition, within the Carnegie family, special thanks go to my good friend Moisés Naím, editor of *Foreign Policy* magazine, for his particular contributions to this project above and beyond the call of duty; to Tom Carothers, for his patience and intelligence; and to Lynne Davidson, for her gentle handling of the editing process.

The book benefited greatly from a series of study group discussions conducted under the auspices of the Carnegie Endowment. Participants in the discussions included U.S. and foreign government officials, business leaders, representatives of multilateral organizations, journalists, officials from non-governmental organizations (NGOs), academics, and other observers. A core group of such individuals attended all of our discussions, which included a general review of the topic as well as individual sessions focusing on each particular case in question. The group was augmented by additional participants with special expertise at each of the case study sessions.

The study group members (see p. 96) generously devoted many hours to reading the discussion papers I prepared. Many helpful ideas, both analytical and prescriptive, emerged from their deliberations. Our discussions were lively and candid and underscored just how important the issues involved are—not only to the U.S. government but also to those on the ground most directly affected by our policies.

Carola McGiffert led the research team behind the book and did a superb job—as she has in every undertaking on which we have worked together. Arlo Devlin Brown and Lillian Rice were the Carnegie staffers assigned to the project, and they produced a veritable mountain of material on which to draw for the discussion papers and the book, while also coordinating the arrangements for our discusssions. Their advice and editorial assistance were much appreciated, as were those of my assistant Jennifer Shore. Jen Sacks, with whom I have worked on every publishing project of which I have been particularly proud in my career, came in at the last minute to pull the pieces together into a coherent whole. With such superb assistance, the detection and correction of any failings in the final product required no special diligence on the part of the author, but I alone am responsible for any the reader might find.

A number of individuals who are current or former members of the Clinton Administration made often generous contributions of their time and ideas to help shape this project. I could not begin to cite them all here, and while I do not wish to suggest that the views in the book represent their views, I want to particularly note the help, advice, or useful insights gained from Tony Lake, Sandy Berger, Mack McLarty, Strobe Talbott, Larry Summers, David Lipton, Bo Cutter, Jeff Garten, Stuart Eizenstat, Joan Spero, Nancy Soderberg, Stanley Roth, Dennis Ross, Hattie Babbitt, Dick Clark, Jim Dobbins, Lauri Fitz-Pegado, Susan Levine, Ann Hughes, Walter Bastian, and Janice Bruce.

We do what we can to promote a more peaceful, prosperous world for our children, and no one is more inspired in this regard than I am. Thanks and love to my daughters, Joanna and Laura.

THE PRICE OF PEACE

INTRODUCTION

On April 3, 1996, thirty-five lives came to a tragic and accidental end during a U.S. government mission aimed at marshaling the power of America's private sector to promote stability in what was once Yugoslavia. But when these American economic peacemakers and those accompanying them on their mission died, there was not a hint of national debate as to why they were there. It was understood that we in the world's richest and most powerful nation have special responsibilities.

In the past four years, we have seen a growing recognition that fostering stability in the post–Cold War world demands that special combination of pragmatic generosity and vision that has distinguished American foreign policy at many of the best moments of "the American century." Once the fighting is stopped or political upheaval is checked, we have repeatedly and increasingly seen that the use or threat of force and diplomatic pressure are not sufficient to keep or construct an enduring peace. Consequently, we find ourselves searching for tools that give those formerly in conflict a stake in a stable future. Those tools are very often economic.

In Haiti, the Middle East, and Bosnia, as well as in Russia, Northern Ireland, Central America, Cambodia, and South Africa, we have come to recognize the importance of using economic levers to help lift countries out of turmoil and keep them out. At the same time, we have discovered that from beginning to end the process of devising economic policies and programs to complement our other post-crisis stabilization efforts has been bedeviled with problems.

The problems begin with the fact that the economic component of intervention in post-crisis situations often is an afterthought. American policy-makers are pressed by the exigencies of conflict to focus principally on the political and the military aspects of the intervention. There is usually the assumption that once we achieve peace, we will do what is necessary to maintain it. But the end of the Cold War precipitated changes beyond the diminution of our leverage with our allies and the elimination of the international dynamics that kept a lid on many regional and internecine conflicts. It also, quite predictably, produced a desire among many in the United States to roll back the internationally oriented spending of the Cold War era. A new isolationism has emerged that enjoys strong adherents among the political leadership of both the Democratic and Republican parties.

Consequently, we find ourselves in a new era in which the threats demand that more thought be applied to whether we should intervene. And, when we do decide to intervene, more thought must be given to the kinds of economic efforts that must come into play to help ensure success. At a time when we are unable and unwilling to underwrite most interventions unilaterally, and when our relative influence within our alliances is diminishing, we increasingly look to allies to share the burdens of peacekeeping. These realities are of course made much more daunting by the turbulent political and military situations that underlie and exacerbate the crises we are trying to resolve. Indeed, we have regularly found that those that we are trying to help have completely different visions from ours as to what "help" means or where it should lead.

There is a growing awareness that these conundrums challenge and occasionally confound U.S. foreign policy-makers. There has been no systematic assessment of the economic dimensions of the foreign policy challenges we face and of the tools we need in order to rise to those challenges.

In this book, I seek to contribute to such an assessment by examining three recent economic interventions by the U.S. government in post-crisis/post-breakthrough situations. I have deliberately limited myself to considering the U.S. government's role; a variety of useful studies already have been made of how the international community responds in such situations. I have chosen Haiti, the Middle East, and Bosnia for the case studies because they best illustrate the range of challenges we face even as they reveal important similarities, thus offering many useful lessons.

This book is addressed to American policy-makers and opinion leaders: to the Executive Branch, in the hope that the study offers a conceptual framework and some practical suggestions for future emergency economic interventions; to the U.S. Congress and the American political community, who must come to realize that unless we are willing to pay the price of peace we will be forced to spend large sums of money on efforts to address humanitarian catastrophes or on the far greater costs of war; and to the broader public, in the hope that it fosters a growing awareness of an important aspect of American foreign policy that for too long has been consigned to the shadows and seen only as an enormous drain on the American taxpayer.

Finally, I dedicate this book to Ron Brown, who was deeply committed to the ideas underlying it, and to the thirty-four peacemakers who died on that plane with him. Like countless others, I miss many of them and think of them often—especially my dear friends and colleagues Bill Morton and Carol Hamilton. May efforts like theirs continue long into the future, honoring their spirit, bettering our world, and enhancing that which is best about America.

David J. Rothkopf
March 1998

*This book is dedicated to the memory of
the men and women who died while promoting peace
when their plane crashed on approach to Dubrovnik Airport
on April 3, 1996*

Ssgt. Gerald Aldrich
Flight Mechanic

Niksa Antonini
Photographer

Dragica Lendic Bebek
Interpreter

Ron Brown
Secretary of Commerce

Duane Christian
Security Officer, U.S.
Department of Commerce

Barry Conrad
Chairman, Barrington
Group

Paul Cushman
Chairman, Riggs
International Banking Corp.

Adam Darling
Confidential Assistant,
U.S. Department
of Commerce

Capt. Ashley Davis
Pilot

Gail Dobert
Deputy Director, Office of
Business Liaison,U.S.
Department of Commerce

Robert Donovan
President, ABB Inc.

Claudio Elia
Chairman, Air and Water
Technologies Corp.

Ssgt. Robert Farrington
Steward

David Ford
President, Interguard Corp.

Carol Hamilton
Press Secretary to the
Secretary of Commerce

Kathryn Hoffman
Senior Adviser for Strategic
Scheduling and Special
Initiatives, U.S. Department
of Commerce

Lee Jackson
U.S. Executive Director,
European Bank for
Reconstruction and
Development

Steve Kaminski
Commercial Counselor,
U.S. Foreign and
Commercial Service

Kathy Kellogg
Confidential Assistant,
Office of Business Liaison,
U.S. Department
of Commerce

Tsgt. Shelly Kelly
Steward

Jim Lewek
Analyst, Central
Intelligence Agency

Frank Maier
Senior Vice President,
Ensearch International
Corp.

Chuck Meissner
Assistant Secretary for
International Trade, U.S.
Department of Commerce

Bill Morton
Deputy Assistant Secretary
for International Economic
Development, U.S.
Department of Commerce

Walter Murphy
Vice President, AT&T
Submarine Systems Inc.

Nathanial Nash
Reporter, *The New York
Times*

Lawrence Payne
Special Assistant, U.S. and
Foreign Commercial
Service, U.S. Department
of Commerce

Leonard Pieroni
Chairman, Parsons Corp.

Capt. Tim Schafer
Pilot

John Scoville
Chairman, Harza
Engineering Co.

Donald Temer
President, Bridge
Housing Corp.

Stuart Tholan
President, Bechtel Europe,
Africa, Middle East, South
Asia

Tsgt. Cheryl Turnage
Steward

Naomi Warbasse
International Trade
Specialist, U.S. Department
of Commerce

Robert Whittaker
Chairman, Foster Wheeler
Energy International Corp.

3

EXECUTIVE SUMMARY

Since the end of the Cold War, U.S. policy-makers have been confronted by a series of regional conflicts in which instability—sometimes the product of military conflict, sometimes the product of traumatic political upheaval—has threatened U.S. interests and those of our allies. These regional crises have threatened our interests by raising the likelihood of wider conflict, by potentially compromising access to key resources, by giving rise to massive humanitarian disasters such as destabilizing refugee flows, or by directly putting at risk our physical security and that of our citizens or allies via ancillary military action or terrorism. However, because these conflicts were localized and frequently seemed remote, decision-makers found it undesirable or impossible to deal with them by introducing significant commitments of U.S. military force for prolonged periods of time. Instead, we have had to devise multifaceted responses that sought to produce stability through the use of a combination of tools and resources—some military, some political, some economic, and all limited by the wariness of the American electorate of extended or costly foreign entanglements.

This book focuses on three such situations that especially commanded the attention of the U.S. government during the first term of the Clinton Administration: Bosnia, the Middle East, and Haiti. In each case, a heavy emphasis was placed on emergency economic intervention as a central tool of our efforts to foster stability. In each, that emergency economic intervention has thus far failed to a significant degree to provide the results that were sought, and in each case that failure has imperiled the overall success of the U.S. mission in the region in question.

Emergency economic intervention is not a new element of U.S. foreign policy. From the Marshall Plan through interventions in Central America, Cambodia, and Kuwait, we have sought to encourage regional stability by giving embattled peoples a material stake in peace. Nonetheless, experience in Bosnia, the Middle East, and Haiti suggests that in the post–Cold War world and the current U.S. political climate, while the importance of such economic interventions has grown, developing effective approaches to intervention has proven to be resiliently difficult. At the same time, it is widely recognized that in places like North Korea and Cuba (see Epilogue, pp. 89-94) situations are developing that may soon demand a U.S.-led response with a significant emergency economic intervention component.

Economic issues will seldom take absolute precedence among our concerns in regional crises. Indeed, one of the conclusions of this book is that they cannot and should not. Physical security must be established first. Political stability must follow. Without these pieces in place, economic efforts will be generally futile, very often wasteful, and sometimes counterproductive. But if peace is to truly take root in the wake of conflict, economic growth is important to making that peace sustainable. Consequently, economic failures can undo military or political successes just as surely as military or political failures can make economic progress impossible.

The U.S. experiences in Haiti, the Middle East, and Bosnia show that emergency economic measures do not currently receive the consideration and/or institutional support that they should. Our overall efforts in each case have suffered as a result.

An analysis of U.S. economic interventions in the three situations considered in this book reveals similarities in the challenges faced, approaches used, tools employed, operational constraints imposed, and outcomes or likely outcomes precipitated by the U.S. intervention. Most strikingly, it reveals that what the U.S. had been doing in the crucial months immediately following interventions in such crises was often ineffective, sometimes wasteful, and invariably inadequate. Timely review of U.S. economic peacekeeping strategies and tactics and of their place in the overall policy structure is called for. American policy-makers need better tools and better thought-out options.

Given the fluid nature of the cases being studied, it is impossible to provide an absolutely up-to-date assessment of each. The in-depth case studies are limited to consideration of the first 18 to 24 months of our post-crisis involvement in each situation; in no case does the period covered extend past the first term of the Clinton Administration. However, as noted earlier, I have provided an Epilogue that attempts to briefly bring the point of view to the present and to look ahead. Recent developments have only amplified my sense that the subject of this book is worthy of close attention and that the conclusions I have reached remain sound.

EMERGENCY ECONOMIC INTERVENTION AND U.S. FOREIGN POLICY

As the world's leading economy, the United States has much to offer if we are willing to commit the necessary resources. But in the current domestic environment, such commitments are unlikely to be made easily. A consensus must be developed as to what emergency economic measures are necessary in post-crisis situations and how to implement them.

What is emergency economic intervention? For the purposes of our discussion, the term means those economic policies and programs undertaken by the United States that are designed to help stabilize a situation that prior to our intervention became volatile for political, military, social, or other reasons. Specifically, it can mean creating jobs to employ former soldiers or police, to reduce unemployment, or to control the flow of refugees. It can mean restoring damaged infrastructure, installing new infrastructure, and supporting the development of necessary public institutions or capital markets. It can mean introducing incentives to develop specific regions or to create trade among different groups or entities. It can mean priming or redirecting or restoring investment flows. It can mean introducing training programs or technical assistance efforts. In every case, it means taking steps that give individuals in a troubled region a palpable, personal stake in the peace—a sense that stability is more in their interest than conflict, and that the new order we support is more in their interest than that which preceded it.

While emergency economic intervention should have longer-term implications for the future development of the country in question, it is about something very different than traditional development economics. This is because the objectives of emergency economics are very much focused on the short- to medium-term. The special economic measures required in emergency economic interventions take on the characteristics of politics more than those of economics. Actions are designed to produce immediate political, social, or security results and to maintain them through the period in which backsliding to renewed crisis is likely or possible. In these cases, as in politics, all economics becomes local.

Projects must be undertaken with specific communities in mind and specific responses sought. A very big component of emergency economics is therefore the production of visible results, because only if the results are visible can they have a political impact. Only if they have political impact can they stimulate the political will to maintain or advance the peace. I call this the "ideology of the light bulb."

Once arms have been laid down, much of the attention of those on the ground returns to the mundane and vital concerns of everyday living: how to get goods to market in Port-au-Prince or Sarajevo when roads are impassable or destroyed, whether or not water comes out of the shower, whether a flip of the switch produces light. But what are the best means of utilizing economic tools to ensure that peace interventions are followed by lasting stability? I will assess the effectiveness of U.S. government efforts to respond to the demands of this "ideology of the light bulb" in three instances: following the U.S.–led intervention to restore democracy to Haiti, after the signing of the Israeli-Palestinian accords, and in post–Dayton agreement Bosnia.

Thus, fundamentally political considerations such as visibility, popular appeal, location of initiatives, timing, etc., must take precedence in emergency economic interventions over traditional economic priorities such as efficiency and value. Yet many of the key economic institutions to which the United States turns in international economic emergencies are steeped in a development ethos that disdains short-term, political fixes. Indeed, failure to understand the need for emergency economic measures as distinct from measures associated with traditional development efforts has plagued U.S. efforts in Haiti, the Middle East, and Bosnia.

CONCLUSIONS

Despite energetic and often creative efforts by policy-makers in the Clinton Administration, I have found that the United States is financially, institutionally, and sometimes temperamentally ill-prepared to face complex conflicts. Our economic efforts in Haiti, the Middle East, and Bosnia—while on-going—have to date produced disappointing results and few real successes. Fortunately, they also have produced useful lessons that may guide our continuing efforts in these regions and can be applied to new crisis zones around the world.

Five major conclusions are drawn from the case studies. Each conclusion is summarized below, then examined in more depth in the chapters that follow.

Conclusion 1: Create an Economic Rapid-Response Capability

Policy-makers invariably undervalue the economic elements of peacekeeping. Economic considerations should be integrated into plans much earlier and their consequences and possibilities weighed more carefully. This can be done by filling the institutional gap within the U.S. government by establishing an economic rapid-response capability.

In each of the three cases considered, the economic component of the peacekeeping/stabilizing process was not given sufficient consideration early enough in the decision-making process. While economic initiatives were not the most important element of our efforts in any of the cases studied, in all three cases military or political progress was seen to be threatened if not followed shortly by economic progress.

While it would be naive and dangerous to expect that U.S. decisions as to whether or not to intervene in crisis situations pivot on economic considerations, it also stands to reason that when we formulate plans and promises we do so on the basis of a realistic assessment of all key factors impacting on the situations at hand—including the economic factors. Policy-makers may choose to proceed with interventions in which sustainable economic recovery may not be a realistic option in the foreseeable future, but they ought to know that when they use expectation-setting rhetoric committing themselves to troop pull-outs, election dates, and target figures. It is dangerous to over-inflate expectations. Crises and euphoria distort perspectives. That is why it is essential to steer clear of both with better, realistic, advance planning, or at least planning done as early as possible.

Policy-makers also need to know where potential economic failures or setbacks will have an impact on security or political initiatives. In all three cases studied, the failure to accept the stark realities of likely problems on the economic front has led to policy errors that have had serious consequences for the realization of our broader foreign policy objectives. The debate over economic reforms has become a fault-line issue separating former Haitian President Jean-Bertrand Aristide from reformers in his party, including his hand-picked successor as president, putting Aristide at odds with the United States and the international community. Israel's closing of its borders to the Palestinian Territories in the wake of terrorist incidents has actually dramatically undercut the Palestinians' already grievous financial state and in turn created a political opportunity for extremist groups such as Hamas. In Bosnia, political impasses have led to an inability to proceed with many major economic programs, rendering the prospects for stability after a NATO withdrawal that much less likely.

If short-term progress or the appearance of progress is enough, then the economic component of an operation can afford to simply *appear* to be sufficient, and that should be understood to be the U.S. objective. If, however, real stability is the objective but is unlikely to be achieved because the cost of economic progress sufficient to support that peace is too high, then top policy-makers must anticipate this stark reality at the outset or be prepared to come to grips with it upon the arrival on our shores of boat people from Haiti—or at the hearings that will be required to justify extending military missions in Bosnia beyond established deadlines.

Economic progress may well be unachievable in *all three* of the cases studied, given spending or other constraints, such as political conflicts or pre-agreed timetables for troop withdrawals, that could preclude success. Above all, policy-makers must know what the U.S. limitations are.

But to determine what those limitations are, a mechanism must be developed within the U.S. government that enables the United States to evaluate situations in which economic intervention may be necessary. We need an economic rapid-response capability akin to that devised for military interventions. This unit would participate in the overall planning of foreign policy initiatives that may require intervention, as well as mobilize and supervise responses.

To institutionalize economic recovery coordinating mechanisms, an office should be established, preferably in the White House, that is responsible for international economic security initiatives. Such an entity would cultivate an institutional memory to ensure that lessons learned are integrated into all future planning. A true inter-agency economic rapid-response team would serve to incorporate economic considerations in long- and short-term foreign policy planning and act as a coordination center for reconstruction activity. Real money, real control, and new incentive programs to stimulate private sector investment are needed. No such capacity now exists.

Continuing with the current assortment of competing, ill-suited, underfinanced, isolated, ad hoc, or short-lived efforts by existing government institutions will only spell failure when it comes to dealing with the complexities of international economic intervention. The result so far, in addition to the paucity of pre-intervention analysis, has been a notable lack of effective tools to deal with the absence of recipient-nation absorptive capacity, as well as with inefficient, improperly targeted, and ineffective aid programs.

The U.S. Agency for International Development (AID)—a major actor in Haiti, the Middle East, and Bosnia—too often proved to be a bureaucratic, slow, and incompetent actor, while several other agencies involved in these efforts, like the Overseas Private Investment Corporation (OPIC), the Export-Import Bank (ExIm), and the Office of the U.S. Trade Representative (USTR), often were constrained from providing valuable assistance by laws designed to serve U.S. interests in normal, commercial—as opposed to emergency—circumstances. *More discretionary latitude* is necessary in emergency or high-priority situations.

In sum, the U.S. needs a dedicated economic rapid-response team with real financial and political support behind it.

Conclusion 2: Master the Local Politics of Emergency Economics

"You can't build an economic house on a political sinkhole." To determine the nature of the ground on which we are attempting to build, the U.S. government must realistically appraise the local political and military situation. It should also assess whether local public and private sector partners in an affected region share our goals, and, if they do not, whether there are effective alternatives to achieve those goals. Conditionality is key.

In Haiti, the Middle East, and Bosnia, the United States has regularly been confounded by the very governments or entities it is trying to help. We need to better understand (and therefore more rigorously analyze) the objectives of our "partners." Furthermore, once aid efforts are under way, we must insist on strict conditionality linking our continued support to performance terms that are narrowly drawn and focused. Aggressive, clearly communicated conditionality from the outset is the only way to motivate reluctant, sometimes inchoate, entities on the ground. While such conditionality may seem to be inconsistent with the pressing need for fast, visible action cited earlier, it is actually directly linked to it because both deal with the underlying political realities. We undertake economic actions to win indigenous political support for the people and policies we want to promote. But we only back the governments in power as long as their views and actions are consistent with our objectives. The cases studied demonstrate that it is crucial for us to be clear about this and for our "partners" to understand it. When they feel the United States will support them at any cost—perhaps because of the amount of domestic political capital the Administration has expended on behalf of operations in a particular situation—then U.S. policy-makers lose control of the effort and risk failure and far greater domestic political damage than the momentary embarrassment caused by standing up to an individual or group they previously have supported. America's actions must be on behalf of America's interests, and no one should be under the illusion that this fundamental necessity will be compromised.

Local government and domestic interest groups can lay waste to international economic reconstruction efforts. The United States must initially and continually thereafter assess the strengths, weaknesses, and difficulties presented by our local partners and other factions on the ground. We must assiduously work to maintain or build local political support for our objectives, or our assistance is not going to be effective. We must also recognize that there are some local factors that are beyond our control and be prepared in some cases to be satisfied with less than 100 percent success. We must also focus what force, money, and influence we have on those elements or parties on the ground that will do the most good. That too requires constant planning and re-assessment. In post-crisis situations, all economics is political as well as local.

The threat to withdraw our support in the face of local refusal to cooperate may come in handy, if we can afford to take that road. When, as in all three cases studied, economic planning is a secondary consideration, such ex post facto conditionality is all but an impossibility. However, if at the outset of an intervention we are careful to position ourselves in such a way that we are not too heavily invested in a particular individual, constraint (such as a timetable), or over-hyped outcome, then we will increase our ability to enforce conditionality. We also increase the chances for success when our international partners share our commitment to the conditions we would set and enforce. It may help to focus our aid less on government entities and more on the private sector within affected regions. In this way, we can maximize our ability to give "around" uncooperative governments to minimize corruption or achieve specific goals.

Having said all of the above, it is essential that we highlight the principal lesson of Bosnia: *If the fundamental internal security and political issues have not been resolved, then most, if not all, economic efforts will ultimately be unsuccessful.* Furthermore, the lack of a cohesive set of purposes and goals on the part of the many nations involved in the effort in Bosnia, as well as the same lack within our own government, demonstrates another way in which politics often trumps economics. Without dealing decisively with the former, we cannot achieve success with the latter. Economics can be a peacekeeper, not a peacemaker.

Conclusion 3: Make a Visible Difference

Rapid deployment of resources to visible projects is key: It builds political will.

Most tools for economic intervention are traditional aid organizations that focus on long-term development. But in emergency interventions it is more important to set short-term, publicizable objectives and meet them—in order to cement the local population's commitment to the new order. Along with achieving measurable and useful objectives, it is vital to communicate these successes both locally and in donor countries. Ensuring project quality is sometimes less important under emergency circumstances than making a maximum impact. Visible results are politically meaningful and ultimately afford longer-term development activity the space to go forward later.

In keeping with an "emergency economics" approach, economic and military initiatives can sometimes be harnessed together. Armies literally can build bridges and engage in other types of immediate projects useful on both a military and an economic level. Moving fast and with high visibility gives more people on the ground a stake in peace. Again, in these situations, all economics become local.

Resources are essential, but resources alone will not suffice. Will and realism must also be added to the mix. Given the budget- and deficit-cutting environment of the U.S. Congress, money is tight and long-term commitments hard to come by. The Administration must re-engage Congress in the battle for greater discretionary aid funding. Mobilizing international money is vital, but it is no substitute for disbursing funds the U.S. can control. Thus it is also crucial that we re-evaluate and restructure our aid spending priorities, so that we can give them a finer focus and target assistance with greater flexibility in fluid situations.

Conclusion 4: Improve U.S. Effectiveness in Multilateral Contexts

We must learn to work more effectively in a multilateral context— and so must the other members of the donor community.

Many key U.S. foreign policy initiatives will require that we influence and often lead multilateral efforts in conjunction with our own. U.S. policy-makers have three options: (1) take the lead when it is essential that the intervention be done precisely to U.S. specifications; (2) learn to lead within multilateral fora when compromise and broad-based support are possible; (3) or, in circumstances when crucial U.S. national interests are not at stake but it is important to do something, contribute and set our expectations at the appropriate low levels.

Multilateral donor structures must be re-evaluated. On the ground, it has become clear that big donor groups need to be driven by a single steering committee of wieldy size. Jockeying for influence within the donor process creates unproductive rivalries, which in some cases are extended to international competition for commercial projects in the region being helped. Moreover, strategic differences must be resolved before an intervention is undertaken.

Conclusion 5: Get the Right Tools

Businesses follow the market, not foreign policy initiatives. New financial tools designed to fund private sector projects in high-risk venues are needed.

Only effective, bottom-line incentives will draw the private sector into post-intervention situations. Therefore we must not expect businesses to do the heavy lifting or to fill the void created by a lack of official resources or will.

Without new programs that create real incentives for companies to undertake considerable risk in transitional or unstable environments, the private sector will not undertake investments in post-intervention situations. It is not enough to maintain OPIC risk insurance programs. No current program was conceived with this particular purpose in mind. Working-capital loan programs at concessional rates would ideally be included in such high-risk investment insurance structures.

Primarily symbolic actions, such as high-profile tours of business leaders to affected regions, are useful in setting and selling the goal. However, real tools are needed to make deals happen. Only after the first stage of government-supported, private sector involvement in target regions has been achieved will businesses be willing and able to go in on their own.

THREE STUDIES IN FRUSTRATION

HAITI

Benchmark for a Hemisphere

Haiti has long held the dubious distinction of being the Western Hemisphere's poorest nation. The economic embargo launched in 1993 to force out the government of Raoul Cedras had a devastating effect on the miserable base from which the nation was working. Per capita income fell from $257 a year in 1991 to $216 in 1993. The island's high unemployment rate soared to 70 percent or more and remained at that level through 1997. Of those among Haiti's seven million people who were employable before the intervention, most worked in subsistence agriculture in a country where less than 10 percent of the land is arable. Eighty percent of the island's people were illiterate. Only 10 percent spoke French, with the rest speaking the island's Creole. The average worker supported ten people with his or her generally very low wage.

The island's light manufacturing sector, which had grown during the 1980s as a consequence of the Haitian people's industriousness, peaked in 1992 with over 125 plants employing 40,000-60,000 employees. This sector was responsible for generating the majority of the country's foreign exchange, as it provided the bulk of Haitian exports. In the months following the embargo, however, the number of Haitians employed within the assembly sector fell to just a few thousand. Journalist Pamela Constable provided an evocative description of the conditions in Haiti in the February 1996 issue of *Current History:*

> During the three years of military rule, conditions in all areas of Haitian life—already the most deprived in the hemisphere—had noticeably worsened. Infectious diseases such as cholera and tuberculosis were rampant, and only 40 percent of the population had access to modern medicine. Free schools were available to only 10 percent of Haitian children. Deforestation and over-farming had severely eroded the land, and the country of 7.5 million had one of the highest population densities in the world.
>
> The economy had shrunk more than 2 percent annually during the 1980s, then plummeted 30 percent during military rule . . . Streets were pocked with craters, most prisons had no water or electricity and some judges were without pencils or paper.

The military government was incompetent, corrupt, and violent (3,000-4,000 deaths were attributed to state violence during the three years of military rule). State companies were allowed to decay to the point that some were inoperable. Others, such as Electricitè d'Haiti, were case studies in inefficiency: Twice as many workers as needed were employed there; half the fuel purchased disappeared before it was used; and half the patrons did not pay for the service they received. Most power-generating facilities were somewhere between rundown and inoperable. What little money was available was wasted or misused. Roads and bridges decayed. Tourism fell from 200,000 visitors a year to almost zero shortly after Jean-Bertrand Aristide's return. When Operation Restore Democracy was initiated in the autumn of 1994, Haiti was an economic wasteland.

A Promising Start, but Declining Prospects for Recovery

The embargo was a double-edged sword. While the U.N.–sponsored action undoubtedly did result in pressure on the military junta running the country, the poorest Haitians suffered its worst effects. Moreover, the negative consequences of the embargo created a great many new challenges for those seeking to help Haiti recover thereafter. U.S. assembly companies that had been in Haiti and then moved out at the request of the U.S. government wanted recompense. Haitian infrastructure deteriorated badly during the embargo and would cost much more to repair. In short, the embargo—arguably useful in the short-term to defeat the military regime—devastated Haiti economically, making the longer-term U.S. objective of restored growth that much more complicated.

It was clear to all that the returning Aristide government would have its work cut out for it on the economic front. As a consequence, President Aristide's government-in-exile undertook a cooperative effort with international advisors to craft an economic plan that would provide sufficient reform to address macroeconomic issues such as controlling inflation, tightening the budget, eliminating impediments to trade, and beginning the process of privatizing parastatal companies. In Paris in August 1994, Aristide's government-in-exile presented to international supporters an economic plan that was a model of good sense and forward thinking. This plan gave international donors the confidence they needed to begin planning their soon-to-be massive aid efforts, debt restructuring, and other steps crucial to Haitian recovery.

Unfortunately, that moment in August, two months before the return of President Aristide, proved to be something of a high-water mark for Haitian economic policy-making. If the plan had been followed in a timely fashion, Haiti might have made substantially more progress to date than it has. But these well-meaning exiles returned to find virtually no apparatus with which to enact their plan. Some efforts, such as that to reduce inflation, were fairly successful, but even these were challenged by populist impulses often championed overtly or covertly by President Aristide himself. In short, economic plans drawn up in the political context of Washington and Paris proved to be far distant from the political reality of Haiti. It can be argued that this should have been better understood by the U.S. policy specialists working on Haiti. It almost certainly was better understood by President Aristide than he let on to his American supporters.

The return of Aristide and the effort to get the junta leaders to depart peacefully was a clear and resounding success. What then?

On the military and political side, there was an answer. The Clinton Administration's Haiti team had put together a thoughtful, detailed political-military plan covering every phase of the operation and ensuring maximum cooperation among the diplomatic, intelligence, and military arms of the U.S. government. On the economic side, in contrast, there was much more of an ad hoc operation. AID had done an enormous amount of work assessing the situation on the ground, liaising with international donors and institutions to lay the foundation for the massive commitments of assistance that were needed. Treasury, too, had been preparing to help Haiti reduce its debt burden—a prerequisite for an IMF stand-by agreement and the beginning of international aid flows. But virtually all the other economic agencies of the U.S. government that could have or should have played a role in Haiti's recovery had been left out of the loop or had been consulted piecemeal as events demanded. Finally, several weeks *after* Aristide's return, it was proposed that a central coordinator and central coordinating mechanism be appointed and established for the U.S. government's Haiti economic recovery efforts. The White House named a senior Commerce official—this author—to lead this initiative, which would involve representatives from the Commerce Department, the State Department, the National Security Council, the Overseas Private Investment Corporation, the Export-Import Bank, the Trade and Development Agency, the Energy Department, the Agriculture Department, the Office of the U.S. Trade Representative, the Treasury Department, the Office of Management and Budget, the Defense Department, the Agency for International Development, and the U.S. Information Agency.

Within eight weeks of Aristide's return, Treasury succeeded in coordinating the forgiveness or paying down of Haiti's outstanding debt, then totaling over $81 million. As a result, the IMF stand-by agreement was signed, and aid money began to flow. In late January 1995, a senior AID official led a delegation to a donors' meeting in Paris that produced a commitment over two years of $1.2 billion (more than Haiti's GDP), including approximately $235 million of U.S. funds. This substantial amount was later raised to approximately $1.6 billion and made Haiti one of the largest per capita recipients of aid dollars in the world.

If the economic recovery plan was the high-water mark for Haitian policy-makers, these first few months were one for U.S. policy-makers. Euphoria surrounded the peaceful return of Aristide; press interest was enormous; and the United States had its largest presence in Haiti at the time. The U.S. military was extremely effective in quickly and gracefully ensuring order and the maintenance of Haitian dignity. The sight of humvees mounted with 50-caliber machine guns in the back and phalanxes of combat-ready soldiers running alongside gave comfort not only to Haitians but also to visiting business people. In early March 1995, the first of a series of high-level trade missions was sent to Haiti from the United States; Deputy Secretary of State Strobe Talbott and Deputy Secretary of Commerce David Barram led the effort, in which over 25 U.S. business leaders participated. Since those heady days, U.S. business interest in trade with Haiti has declined rapidly, mostly due to Aristide's public and private opposition to economic reform.

During 1996, the economic policy fissures began to widen. Between March and July, six off-duty police officers were assassinated; central bank chief Leslie Delatour was robbed; and, in July 1996, the United States responded to the growing unrest in Haiti by sending over 150 troops to provide security to Aristide's successor, René Préval, as well as to regain order in the streets. It is telling, if not chilling, that the rallying cry of the dispossessed in Haiti today is the same as it was under military rule: "Lavi Che!" which means, roughly translated from Creole, "We can't afford to live." And, in early 1997, in response to the prospect of privatization and further reforms, activist René Civil led a nationwide strike protesting "foreign interference in Haiti."

Although the situation in Haiti remains fluid, Aristide has become a major obstacle to real progress. Despite the opposition, President Préval appears to be making some of the tough decisions that his predecessor did not. Préval is showing considerably more assertiveness in terms of advancing privatization and ensuring fiscal responsibility, including refusing to print new money to pay the bills. With regard to privatization, Préval has taken a tough stand, at least in rhetoric, stating that "in 10 years, [state-owned companies] have been unable to modernize. Now for them it is sudden death." Bills to enable privatization have also finally been passed—but the process will start with the least controversial and important state industries (the flour mills and cement businesses). Nonetheless, Aristide-led political opposition to their implementation has remained fierce, resulting (as noted above) in general strikes in early 1997, followed later by the resignation of Prime

Minister Rosny Smarth. Aristide, for his part, has taken to publicly denouncing the authors of economic reform provisions as "American imperialists."

THE MIDDLE EAST

Next Door to a Relative Paradise

Situated in the tiny sliver of land wedged between Israel and the Mediterranean Sea, the Gaza Strip is an accident of the geopolitical mismanagement that characterized the end of the imperial era. Gaza is the largest of the scores of official and unofficial cities and towns in the region that teem with Palestinian refugees, their children, and their children's children. Well over half of the more than 800,000 residents of the strip are the descendants of Palestinians who found themselves without a home in 1948. By any definition, Gaza is squalid; for many, finding clean water or a dependable power supply is just a dream.

The story is somewhat different in the other sector of the new Palestinian territory, the West Bank. Underdevelopment still reigns in the West Bank, but many of the inhabitants live where their families have lived for decades if not centuries. Compared with Gaza, the West Bank enjoys fifteen times as much space, has a border with a nation other than Israel, and now is the putative capital of a new political entity, the Palestinian Authority (PA), and the would-be forerunner of a nation—inchoate, fragile, and invested with much hope.

Gaza and the West Bank make up the whole of an experiment in which the state of Israel, in order to achieve peace, has started down the path toward ceding lands it won in wars of self-preservation to the majority Palestinian population, many of whom have been Israel's sworn enemies since its inception almost half a century ago. Like the previous political solutions tested on the peoples of the region, this one offers hope not only for the end of armed conflict but also for a brighter economic future for the Palestinians in the PA, who need only look across the Green Line to see the Middle East's most prosperous, technologically advanced democracy.

For many in the Territories, of course, that hope is tempered by bitter experience. Past political "solutions" from the Balfour Declaration through modern times have produced only more conflict. The peace based on the Oslo agreements suffers from some grievously apparent flaws. Partitioned nations seldom flourish. Gaza is surrounded by Israel and the sea. Its trade can come only at the sufferance of a state that views many in Gaza as a security threat. The future of the West Bank also depends on strong relations with Israel, as well as with Jordan—a neighbor whose moderate King suffers from cancer and whose future is far from assured. Many in Israel oppose the land-for-peace deal that produced the Oslo and Taba agreements that form the foundation upon which the new peace is being built. Many within the Palestinian Territories similarly oppose the deal and have vowed to undermine it and the "moderate" government promised by PLO leader Yasir Arafat.

History and economics do not make the picture much more encouraging. Gaza, suffering from urban density without the needed infrastructure to support it, has a population that is growing at 4 percent a year. Both the West Bank and Gaza have little in the way of internal resources beyond a talented and energetic people. Since the Territories were occupied by the Israelis following the 1967 war, they have grown increasingly dependent on Israel for their survival. Estimates suggest that at their peak, prior to the recent string of border closings and upheavals, perhaps as many as 70 percent of the workforce of the Territories crossed the Green Line into Israel to get to their jobs. These people, perhaps 125,000 in number, produced almost half of the GDP of the Territories. Thus the Territories were heavily dependent on access to Israel for survival. At the same time, their level of subsistence was far below that of the economy on which they depended and to which so many daily traveled. By 1992, the combined GDP of Gaza and the West Bank amounted to only 6.7 percent of Israel's.

Palestinian isolation has been exacerbated over the past decades for several additional reasons. Israeli occupation was the primary reason that these Territories felt cut off from the Arab world. But when Arafat made the fateful choice to back Saddam Hussein in the Gulf War, not only did the PLO lose the crucial financial assistance of many in the Arab world, but Palestinian employment opportunities throughout the region and notably in Kuwait also were cut off. Then, first in the wake of the intifada and later as a consequence of terrorist bombings aimed at disrupting the peace process, the Israelis began regularly to shut down the Green Line to contain Palestinians and possible terrorists in their midst. The result was of course economically devastating to the Palestinians.

Today, unemployment in the Palestinian Territories ranges from 40-60 percent. Only 5-7 percent of the Territories' income comes from domestic production. Of the Territories' two million people, approximately one-sixth live at or below the poverty line, and incomes average around $600 per year. Furthermore, most of the Palestinian people are very young: 70 percent of the Palestinians in Gaza are under 24 years of age. As the Israeli government already has found, youth, poverty, and political tension are a volatile mixture. The goal of the economic peacekeepers who descended on the region in the wake of the 1993 Oslo agreement was to defuse this time bomb before it undid the best efforts of the world's diplomats and sent the region back into a cycle of violence and retribution.

A Fragile Moment

Few international situations are entirely comparable to the unrest and conflict that has followed the creation of the state of Israel in 1948. Certainly no issue other than the Cold War itself has so dominated U.S. foreign policy throughout the past half century. From President Harry Truman's recognition of Israel in the first days after its independence, through our aid initiatives in the Six-Day War and the Yom Kippur War, to the provision of Patriot missiles during the Gulf War, America has been Israel's essential, unwavering ally. Indeed, the peace process was made possible by the fact that it is now an accepted fundamental of American policy that the United States will defend and preserve the state of Israel under any circumstances. Even Israel's sworn enemies have come to recognize that a powerful Israel allied with the world's sole superpower is an inevitable fact of life with which they must come to grips.

Consequently, the parties to the peace talks have gone beyond sterile debate over whether Israel has the right to exist to equally contentious yet substantive questions regarding Israel's borders and how to treat the Palestinian peoples who once shared the land that is now occupied by the Jewish state. American presidents and secretaries of state have made the peace discussions that would resolve these last questions central concerns since the 1970s, beginning with the shuttle diplomacy of Henry Kissinger, carrying through to the Camp David Accords, and continuing with the extraordinary efforts of Secretary of State Warren Christopher in the region during the first Clinton Administration.

The September 13, 1993, Middle East Peace Accords signing ceremony on the South Lawn of the White House was one of the galvanizing moments of recent history. The handshake between sworn enemies, the transformation of soldiers and terrorists into peacemakers, and the commitment to working together toward peace were the stuff of great drama. But it was also clear even to casual observers that, given the deep-seated nature of the hostilities, the wariness of the signatories, and the absence of key players such as Syria from the mix of peacemakers, much work still needed to be done. The hesitation with which Yitzhak Rabin greeted the outstretched hand of Arafat illustrated this better than a volume of journal articles could hope to do.

The situation confronting U.S. economic planners following the Oslo agreements was different from that in Haiti or Bosnia in a number of respects. Our relations with the local governments were long established, even if they were going through a profound change. We also had a history of committing significant financial resources to the region in the forms of both military and more traditional foreign aid. In the wake of the Camp David Accords, we had even made a commitment to economic growth as a key element of our peacekeeping efforts, dedicating $5 billion per year to supporting development in Israel and Egypt. Due in part to those efforts and in part to the Camp David Accords—and in large part to the industry of the Israeli people—Israel also had made a remarkable economic turnaround, opening its markets, developing a reputation as a world leader in key technologies, and turning desert into farmland. Furthermore, the Palestinians' standard of living, however deplorable, was well above that of the Haitians—only a sixth of all Palestinians lived in absolute poverty as compared with nine-tenths of all Haitians—and the Palestinian people were well known for their own entrepreneurial gifts and for their high level of education.

The economic prospects for the new Palestinian entity looked even brighter when considered in the light of certain factors: an international donor commitment of almost two and a half billion dollars during the five years from 1993 to 1998; the entry of neighboring Jordan into the peace process, which opened up new opportunities along the eastern border of the West Bank; and the fact that the Palestinians only had to look north to chaotic, shattered Lebanon, where even the Lebanese were beginning to attract significant sums of investment.

Despite these hopeful developments, the problems that had divided Arab and Jew in Israel were traceable to antiquity, and Palestinians and Jews had been each other's sworn enemies since the restoration of the state of Israel and before. Few should therefore be surprised that violence has overtaken diplomacy and set back economic progress. The assassination of Rabin and subsequent terrorist attacks and Israeli counter-measures have cast a dark shadow over the efforts of peacemakers—and one vital factor in the resurgence of groups like Hamas has been the absence of tangible economic progress for the Palestinian people. The Oslo agreements have not improved their lives, and, feeling the pain, many have proven to be more responsive in recent months to the all too familiar call of the radicals. At the same time, the United States has found it difficult to criticize the Israeli tactics that have exacerbated the Palestinians' economic problems. Security does take precedence and, as in the case of Bosnia, when security issues are unresolved, economic efforts falter, and the promises associated with them ring hollow.

BOSNIA

War and Ruin

The numbers that illustrate the story of Bosnia—a conflict that languished for so long on the international back burner—are staggering. Virtually everyone in the fractured nation paid a price. During the fighting among Serbs, Croats, and Bosniaks, 145,000-200,000 people were killed, and at least as many were injured. More than half of almost four and a half million people who lived in Bosnia before the war began were displaced from their homes, and more than a quarter left the country. Nine out of ten who live there now depend at least in part on humanitarian assistance to survive. This in itself is a sign of the importance of outside economic intervention in the post-conflict period—if that is how the situation today can be described. It is also, however, a sign of how dire the circumstances were and how far the country has to come to recover its footing. By the time the Dayton Peace Accords were signed, virtually every sinew of society—political, social, economic, and religious—had been rent by war, savagery, and recrimination. A community that prided itself on cosmopolitan tolerance—a productive European society—had collapsed.

In the case of Bosnia, the nuts and bolts of recovery would have been daunting even if all the Bosnians who survived the war had remained where they were when it began. Over 500 villages were completely destroyed by the war. Over 60 percent of the housing stock has been damaged—and a third of that, totally destroyed. Half of all factories have been wrecked, as have half the schools. A third of all medical facilities have sustained serious damage. One World Bank estimate set the total cost of restoring Bosnia to its pre-conflict economic state at $25 billion dollars.

The pain of the blows described here was compounded by the fact that, unlike the people of Haiti or Gaza, prior to the war the people of Bosnia had lived an especially good life for the region. In 1991, the 4.3 million citizens of Bosnia had a per capita GDP of $1,900. The national GDP was $8.3 billion. The external debt-to-GDP ratio was 23 percent.

By the end of 1996, the GDP had fallen over 75 percent, to around $2 billion. The GDP per capita had consequently also fallen, to $500. External debt was now 125 percent of GDP, and two-thirds of that—over $3 billion in debt—was in arrears. All this exists in a country where state and local institutions are somewhere between absent and feeble and, as noted earlier, many leaders have resisted the leap from state socialism to market economies that Central European countries have now struggled to make for over half a decade.

23

A Fatal Lack of Interest

When the seeds of the conflict that devastated Bosnia were sown, the great world powers were looking the other way. Indeed, the relatively offhand attitude with which the international community regarded the breakdown of the former Yugoslavia exacerbated the problem. Germany pushed through recognition of Croatia and Slovenia despite the reservations of its close allies. America and the other leading nations responded half-heartedly, with grudging recognition of the new states or with no action at all—sending a message to both would-be nation-builders and unscrupulous exploiters of nationalistic tensions that the future shape of Yugoslavia was not a high priority.

Notably, the crisis in Bosnia has failed to mobilize anything like the U.S. domestic political support that exists for action in Haiti and the Middle East. Pro-Israeli Jews, pro-Palestinian Arabs, and pro-Haitian Caribbeans and African-Americans are very well organized, recognized political forces in key communities in America and on the national level. There was no comparable group with an interest in the Bosnia crisis, and even many of those who were concerned saw Bosnia as a problem for the European Community to handle. As a consequence, U.S. intervention in Bosnia was much more politically risky for President Clinton, and he entered the situation tightly constrained by the public's low level of tolerance for high-cost involvement in the former Yugoslavia.

Nonetheless, the nature and success of intervention in Bosnia is now seen by U.S. foreign policy-makers as crucial to answering a number of important questions: How does this operation influence the development of NATO? How does it influence the development of relations with the Islamic world and with Russia? And how well can we rise to the challenges of post–Cold War leadership in a situation abounding in ambiguities, ambivalence, paradoxes, and conundrums?

In the time since the Dayton Accords were reached, the risks taken by the President have been compounded for reasons much like those dogging the White House in Haiti and the Middle East. Those we were trying to help not only did not cooperate but periodically obstructed progress. Political institutions in the new states of the region failed to coalesce as votes were contested; local power struggles overshadowed debate; and little attention seemed to be paid to real institution-building or to the rule of law. Dayton Accords provisions were flouted. War criminals remained free. Refugees were denied passage to their homes. Prerequisites for economic aid flows were ignored. Consequently, estimates suggest that, through the end of the first term of the Clinton Administration, Bosnia had received just 10 percent of the aid dollars that were seen to be necessary for total reconstruction and perhaps only a quarter of the total expected to be disbursed during the initial period of rebuilding. Furthermore, in the wake of such faltering efforts, international investment is on hold in Bosnia—as it is in the Palestinian Territories and in Haiti—due to rising tensions and doubts about the future of peacekeeping efforts in the region.

Indeed, despite intense and sometimes heroic efforts on the part of American officials to seek sustainable peace in each of these three regions, even casual analysis results in an unavoidable conclusion: U.S. efforts have failed to restore economic hope or confidence among either the victims of past instability or the international private sector, yet both must play crucial roles in fostering the future growth of these troubled lands.

CONCLUSION 1: CREATE AN ECONOMIC RAPID-RESPONSE CAPABILITY

Policy makers regularly undervalue the economic elements of peace-keeping. Economic considerations should be integrated into plans much earlier and their consequences and possibilities should be weighed more carefully. This can be done by filling the institutional gap within the U.S. government by establishing an economic rapid-response capability.

We must carefully assess what the economic elements of any foreign policy program are and, at the same time, review our willingness and capability to effectively realize desired policy goals. And as we evaluate economic issues from the start, we must recognize their relative importance to reaching the goals. With that analytical basis, we can either apply the necessary resources or prepare ourselves to accept the alternatives.

To engage in such an analysis, the institutionalization of economic recovery coordinating mechanisms is called for. An Office for International Economic Security Initiatives should be established, preferably in the White House, ideally within the National Security Council. It should be run by someone with sufficient seniority to be able to coordinate the activities of all the relevant agencies of the U.S. government. The establishment of this office would not only enhance the effectiveness of future coordination efforts; it would ensure the cultivation of a currently unavailable institutional memory. The lessons of emergency economic intervention should be learned and adjusted as appropriate for future undertakings. Ad hoc approaches are neither effective nor necessary. In the years ahead (see Epilogue, p. 89), emergency economic efforts will continue to often be centrally important to U.S. foreign policy—not only in the three cases discussed here but also in likely upcoming challenges such as the reunification of the Koreas and the transformation of post-Castro Cuba.

With an institution for emergency economic coordination in place within the U.S. government, policy-makers will be better able to answer questions that are key to the success of any intervention: What are our goals and interests? Do we wish to alter perceptions in a given situation, or do we want to affect underlying conditions and promote long-term change? Either can be a legitimate motivation, depending on the circumstances. What the U.S. cannot afford is to speak and act without regard for economic realities, making promises we cannot keep.

The fact is that ultimately our interventions in troubled nations or regions will be judged not by whether or not we restore stability, but by whether that stability is sustainable. And stability without hope, without the creation of economic opportunities, is just another name for the pause that precedes further conflict.

HAITI

To many, intervention in Haiti—a tiny, impoverished island nation with no military capability or economic attractions of any consequence to the United States—seemed a questionable allocation of America's national resources. Yet Haiti was important to politicians because it was important to two key special interest groups: Black Americans and Floridians. America's Black population, a key part of the Democratic Party's base, cared about Haiti for a number of reasons— some because there were Haitians among them (approximately one million), others because they felt that U.S. indifference toward the plight of this island was an extension of American racism, and still others because of historical concerns about conditions on the island. The second special interest group was the population of Florida. Not only was Florida— Dade County in particular—home to the world's largest concentration of Haitians outside Haiti, but it was also the dreamed-of destination of Haitians who took to the high seas in search of a better life. As one member of Congress from Florida put it: "For Florida, Haiti is a local issue." In addition, and perhaps most important, Florida is a crucial swing state in presidential politics and was a battleground state in the 1996 presidential election. Florida's "local" issues have a tendency to very quickly become "national" issues.

Add to the mix a group of high-profile entertainers like Julia Roberts, Jonathan Demme, and Danny Glover, and high-drama activists like TransAfrica president Randall Robinson, whose hunger strike in support of decisive action was probably the single most galvanizing event for an Administration that had been uncertain about its next move. These people were significant in American politics because they made the story "photogenic at home."

The Clinton Administration cited the restoration of Haitian democracy as the paramount reason for the economic embargo and later for the mobilization of troops, which became the most visible manifestations of U.S. policy. Clearly, the restoration of democracy to a nation from which it was wrested by a military coup sends an important message—especially when that nation is so close to U.S. borders. However, the reason stated for any intervention generates the criteria by which success or failure of the initiative will be judged. And the fact is that the Administration's underlying goals for the intervention in Haiti were domestic and political: to stop the flow of boat people to Florida and to assure Black Americans that U.S. foreign policy tools were available to support their interests. Consequently, nothing short of decisive intervention and enduring stability would be sufficient to satisfy the political demands on the Administration.

When Emergency Economics Gets Put on the Back Burner

The Clinton Administration's efforts to support the return of the democratically elected president to Haiti and to help ensure that democracy would take root in that country were successful in a number of important respects. It is beyond dispute that diplomacy won a return of Aristide that was largely without bloodshed; that the much-loved leader of the Haitian people was restored to his rightful position; and that Haitians now live without many of the fears that dominated daily life for years. It is also true that elections were held—flawed to be sure, but elections nonetheless—leading to the first peaceful transfer of power in the country's almost 200-year history. These are significant achievements. America's role in making them possible is undeniably to our credit and sends a strong message about our commitment to the rule of law in our immediate neighborhood.

That said, in our efforts to restore democracy to Haiti, the United States was unable to respond effectively to the demands of "the ideology of the light bulb." Before Aristide was returned to the presidency in 1993, electric power was available in Port-au-Prince only two to four hours a day. It was unavailable in virtually every other city, town, or hamlet in the country. All electricity was cut off at 7:00 p.m. There were 60,000 phone lines on the island—a telephone density per person of approximately four telephones per thousand people—a penetration roughly equivalent to that in the Central African Republic. Safe drinking water was scarce. Roads and bridges were unusable. The managers of the nation's infrastructure were often inefficient, often ineffective, and sometimes corrupt. But the managers were protected by the fact that theirs were national industries, and the jobs they held, sinecures.

It has been four years since Aristide's restoration to power. While improvements slowly have been made, the general economic situation today is roughly the same for the vast majority of Haitians as it was the day the U.S. troops arrived. Most still do without power or telephones. And while some limited initial steps toward privatization finally have been taken, it is likely to be years before the nation's infrastructure "industries" are reformed or their service improved. Indeed, a national debate over the merits of much needed privatization divides the country and has introduced significant tensions into the relationship between

Haitian leaders and their would-be supporters in the international community.

In the Haiti case, many key economic issues were allowed to fester and were addressed late if at all. Despite the fact that the U.S. embassy in Port-au-Prince was, like all U.S. embassies, severely understaffed on the economic and commercial side, the U.S. government had the benefit of excellent reporting on economic conditions. However, the lack of clout among economic policy-makers within the State Department and the secondary role that the National Economic Council plays vis-à-vis the National Security Council exacerbated these problems, always consigning economic issues to secondary status even when they were of primary importance. While the top Administration officials responsible for Haiti ultimately made an effort to compensate for this, none of the changes have been institutionalized, and thus the battle to bring economic policy considerations alongside military and political considerations in the planning process is constantly being re-fought.

Lurching Toward Effectiveness

Once the White House did establish an interagency economic Steering Group for Haiti, chaired by the author from December 1994 through January 1996, it suffered from the fact that it was not run out of the White House, won mixed support from the various agencies called upon to participate in its activities, and had no capacity to influence budget decisions. Instead, it worked within already established, often inappropriate, spending parameters. What is more, this committee was temporary in nature. Not only did it lack sufficient authority, it was unable to pass on what it learned, since there was no institutional successor. When I departed the chairmanship to return to the private sector, the committee was disbanded, and the economic recovery effort returned to ad hoc coordination.

The Overseas Private Investment Corporation (OPIC), which provides political risk insurance and offers an on-lending program, was notably unable to move quickly but also unable to help many of the firms that were most severely hit by the embargo, since their balance sheets no longer met OPIC creditworthiness requirements. (OPIC also was unable to lend to certain sectors for fear that U.S. critics in the Congress and elsewhere would accuse the agency of acting in violation of laws precluding it from creating jobs abroad at the possible expense of U.S. workers.) According to Susan Levine, then Vice President of OPIC, the agency could not ignore commercial criteria and thus was not the right tool for Haiti. (As it turns out, this argument was substantially reiterated when OPIC was asked to participate in efforts in Bosnia and the Palestinian Territories.) That begs the question: What *are* the right kinds of economic tools for countries like Haiti, and where are they to be found?

They do not seem to exist within the current structure of the U.S. government's trade financing agencies. Like OPIC, ExIm was the wrong tool for Haiti. ExIm was completely precluded from activity in Haiti due to Haiti's bottom-of-the-barrel credit rating. The Trade Development Agency (TDA), which funds feasibility studies, moved slowly into Haiti, citing the relative commercial merits of other uses for its very limited budget. Even casual observers came away strongly of the opinion that there was an institutional gap among U.S. programs and a need for the kind of programs that could induce risk-averse business people into markets when it was clearly in the U.S. national interest to do so. The "herd effect" can work to encourage or discourage investment, because potential investors look to see who else has gone into or stayed out of—a country before deciding whether to do so themselves.

OPIC, ExIm, USTR, and other agencies also were constrained from providing valuable assistance due to laws or regulations designed to serve U.S. interests in normal commercial circumstances. In emergency situations, there must be institutions willing to give some money away and to conduct assistance on less stringent bases than those upon which commercial endeavors are conducted (both in terms of creditworthiness and in terms of the efficiency of the recipients' practices). Seeking presidential waivers is usually considered politically unpalatable or impossible. Thus new legislation is required to permit those institutions to engage in the kinds of programs that post-intervention situations demand.

In addition, it would help if the U.S. government continued to develop military-civilian economic cooperation in post-intervention situations. The rest of the government can learn a great deal about how to approach these situations from studying the planning, organization, and execution of U.S. military operations like Operation Restore Democracy. Moreover, Haiti illustrated the significant contribution to civilian needs that the military can make in the course of performing its peacekeeping function. In Haiti, cooperative efforts took a variety of forms ranging from the involvement of the Army Corps of Engineers in helping restore Haiti's power, road, and bridge infrastructures to the Army's active role in helping support Haiti's nascent police force. More study should be done of other areas of potential cooperation and technical assistance, such as port management, air traffic control, coastal patrol, border enforcement, training, and other areas in which the military has great expertise.

An Absence of Absorptive Capacity

While AID and other foreign aid agencies did yeoman groundwork to create a bureaucracy and distribution mechanisms in Haiti to enable the country to absorb the over $1.2 billion given by the international community for rebuilding and revitalization, it is clear that their efforts came up short.

Funding was provided for the formation of a special team in the Prime Minister's office that was to ensure that assistance moneys were efficiently deployed; but the team took months to get on its feet. Once it did, it suffered myriad other problems, including lack of support from the office of the President, differing demands from Haitian special interest groups, lack of bureaucratic infrastructure in virtually all Haitian agencies, and a developing budget crisis that came in the wake of Haiti's failure to reach agreement on the terms of an International Monetary Fund Structural Adjustment Credit (SAC). This failure also held up other financing and sucked all available cash into "essential" government services. Furthermore, because of standard operating procedures within agencies such as AID, and because of the absence of appropriate government infrastructure in Haiti, much of the available aid money was administered by non-governmental organizations. This kept the funds out of the ineffective and sometimes corrupt hands of the Haitian government, but it also made it difficult to ensure that funds were being directed toward the concerns of most pressing interest to U.S. policymakers, i.e., high-visibility projects that could show the Haitian people that progress was being made.

Inefficient, Badly Targeted, and Ineffective Aid Programs

While AID played an absolutely crucial role in the U.S.–Haiti Economic Recovery Initiative, there were many problems associated with that agency's efforts. First, because AID was in a budget fight for its life, funds were limited, and the flexibility was virtually absent to move funds into new accounts to address changing situations on the ground. In addition, many Haitians were uncomfortable with the AID management team on the ground. More fundamentally, AID doctrines are drawn heavily from the development philosophies of the 1970s and 1980s; they place emphasis on important issues such as health, literacy, sanitary conditions, security, elections, and the other concerns of "civil society." While AID programs addressing some of these concerns—most notably security and job creation—had important short-term impacts, and while the others are important from a humanitarian perspective, the overall impact of AID efforts was far less than it could have been had more money been focused on fewer programs with more visible results and more carefully considered political consequences.

That is not to say that the AID efforts were not worthy undertakings. But in a time of tight money, AID resisted efforts to refocus spending on the infrastructure needs cited by would-be investors, moved too slowly to produce results in the timeframe that would have had maximum political impact, and relied heavily on bureaucratic impulses when speed, flexibility, and creativity were called for. Nonetheless, the AID efforts were home to the vast majority of the U.S. budget that was available to the Haiti Economic Recovery Initiative. Finally, when AID was successful, as when it created tens of thousands of acutely needed short-term jobs, the agency fundamentally failed to effectively communicate these successes to the Haitian people. This was perhaps the most serious problem of all in a situation in which it was in the U.S. interest to win popular support for the changes that had been wrought.

Moreover, a contentious relationship between the Administration and Congress resulted in an increasing number of caveats, constraints, and burdens being placed on would-be policy-makers. The Congress blocked or held funds, undertook investigations, sent conflicting messages, and, perhaps inevitably, made the Administration's already difficult job that much more difficult.

Mobilizing the U.S. Government

The Haiti Economic Recovery Steering Group met and quickly identified a list of steps that could be taken by the U.S. government to help stimulate trade and investment. The goal was to make a "visible difference." This goal reflected the principle behind the "ideology of the light bulb" and was adopted in an effort to give the Haitian people a sense of progress and the consequent benefits that could come from re-establishing democratic administration. It should be noted, however, that virtually all of the U.S. aid directed to Haiti did not go through this steering group but rather passed solely through AID, which focused on traditional development programs such as those noted earlier. Thus, all other agencies were forced to find money in tight budgets for short-term, high-visibility efforts, and virtually none have contingency budgets for such tasks, despite the increasing importance of such efforts in peace-keeping situations. The steering group itself was given what was called a "vital" mission but essentially zero discretionary dollars with which to accomplish it.

The list of actions called for by the Economic Recovery Steering Group included:

- Creation of a series of business and investment development missions by the U.S. Department of Commerce, focusing on key sectors selected for their importance to Haiti and the possibility of swift action.

33

- Creation by Commerce of a U.S.–Haiti Business Development Committee, a "permanent" organization chaired by the Haitian Minister of Finance and a top Commerce official and including 25 American and 25 Haitian business leaders. This group was designed to provide the kind of four-way dialogue between public and private sectors that is so essential to setting priorities.
- Establishment by Commerce of the first full-time commercial office in Haiti and the staffing of that office by a top contract employee from the United States.
- Establishment of Haiti Fax and Internet hotlines providing information to U.S. businesses.
- Finalization of a $50-million OPIC on-lending facility through the Bank of Boston (later shifted to Citibank after the Bank of Boston office closed). This facility ultimately approved over $32 million to 25 different companies. (It should be noted that many in the business community expressed frustration with this program on many levels. First, it took somewhat longer than planned to get started, and when it did, it was only through one bank, the Bank of Boston. Getting a second bank involved took so long that the first one had, as noted, closed by the time a second one had signed on. In addition, OPIC lending rules prohibited loans to companies that might be creating jobs that would take the place of U.S. workers. The rules specifically cut out one of the biggest categories of potential investors, apparel manufacturers, who also happened to be among those most seriously hurt by the embargo. Several of these complained that credit requirements were too strict, though this proved to be a rather limited problem. What is clear, however, is that what wary investors really required was a greater incentive to go in than the commercially oriented OPIC or any other U.S. government institution was capable of offering.)
- Treasury secured a letter of interest from the Haitian government to begin the process of making Haiti eligible for Section 936 funds. This required the beginning of the process leading up to a Tax Information Exchange Agreement. The later death of the 936 program makes this effort moot.
- Agriculture inaugurated a GSM-102 Program providing export credit guarantees to help finance imports of a variety of U.S. agricultural products. While two banks sought approval to participate in the program, approval delays were lengthy, reflecting the varying sense of urgency about Haiti in different branches of the U.S. government.
- ExIm was prodded to make some financing available in Haiti but explained that it could not due to Haiti's low credit rating. ExIm

might have considered providing a guarantee service, but instead sought to avoid controversy by steering clear of the issue and the country altogether.

- USTR entered into discussions with Haiti about a variety of issues: a bilateral textile agreement, waiving certain restrictions on the use of sugar quotas, and helping with Haitian entry into the World Trade Organization (WTO), which occurred in January 1996. The Haitian government failed to move as it should have in each of these areas, failing to ratify WTO membership in Parliament, failing to act to use the existing textile ceilings that were available while arguing that higher ones were needed, and failing to take steps to ensure that the sugar quota waiver would benefit any Haitian beyond a single family. The Haitian government also failed to take any action or express its intent with regard to moving ahead with a Trade and Investment Framework Agreement (even though such agreements are in place between the United States and all countries in the Hemisphere except Haiti and Cuba).

- The Department of Energy offered technical assistance to help the Haitians with their severe energy problems and worked closely with the Army Corps of Engineers to identify maintenance and repair goals.

Beyond pressing for the above-mentioned efforts, the steering committee played a number of other roles. These included beginning the systematic gathering and analysis of information about Haiti's economy and recovery efforts and the dissemination of that analysis to top policy-makers throughout the U.S. government and Congress. In addition, and even more significantly, the committee began to take on the role of trouble shooter. For example, the Committee's Chair and the U.S. Ambassador to Haiti intervened in an attempt to persuade President Aristide not to more than triple the country's minimum wage, an action that would have been highly inflationary, damaging the budget and sending a very unsettling message to foreign investors while diminishing Haitian competitiveness. As a direct result of this intervention, President Aristide raised the minimum wage only to a level commensurate with inflation (doubling rather than tripling the minimum wage).

At first, the political conundrum presented by Aristide's populist policies and foot-dragging on economic reform was not deemed central, because the privatization process required a variety of steps that were taking place, albeit slowly. AID allocated funds to the International Finance Corporation (IFC) to undertake a study of privatization options and offer recommendations to the Haitian government. This study took months to conduct, and when it was concluded, its results were not shared with the U.S. government because AID had accepted terms to its funding arrangement whereby, despite having paid for the study, the U.S. government was not to be privy to its results. This arrangement gave the Haitian government the opportunity to offer any number of self-serving interpretations of its results.

Some in the U.S. government believed Aristide when he promised imminent progress and felt that, because of budget pressure, progress would be made, because the IMF Structural Adjustment Credit (SAC) was so important that the Aristide government would do whatever was necessary to secure it. Others sensed a different feeling on the part of the Haitians—one that was even articulated in conversations with some of the more candid leaders in Haiti. "Look," they said, "there are two presidential elections coming up. We know that. Ours and yours. Can President Clinton afford to let fail this experiment, on which billions have been spent? You need us more than we need you. Don't forget— our people are accustomed to misery."

The international community hanged tough on the issue of SAC conditionality. The Haitians dragged their feet throughout the process of discussions, first failing to prepare for meetings with the international financial institutions, later stonewalling, still later simply not holding meetings any more. Time passed. As the Haitian election drew close, everything was put on hold—the main focus was on ensuring that Aristide would step down as planned and that the elections would be credible. They were—if only barely.

A new government took over. Yet, six months into fiscal 1996, there was no budget and no SAC; the Haitian government was running on empty, literally living on foreign reserves; and investors were sitting firmly on their hands. The final vote on privatization did not take place until late 1996, and, as of the end of 1997—over three years after Aristide's return—only the country's long shut down and dilapidated flour mill had been privatized. Indeed, the privatization issue remains politically divisive within Haiti. With all but a handful of foreign troops gone from the island, there is great uncertainty in the business community about the future of Haiti. The CEO of the largest U.S. employer in Haiti said in early January 1996, after several of his top executives had been roughed up by thugs on their way home from work: "I'm worried. I've been in Haiti for years, through good times and bad, and this is the worst it's ever been. I've put a hold on all our contracts in Haiti. We're going to wait and see." Nothing that has happened since encourages optimism. "In fact," he says, "it's only got worse. There's no government there now, except Aristide's clique and, frankly, they've become the problem."

THE MIDDLE EAST

A lthough enmities in this region were ancient, the facts clearly show that the efforts to help support peace through economic development in the new Palestinian Territories had many distinct advantages over similar initiatives in Haiti and Bosnia—not the least among them being the fact that Americans accepted that vital U.S. interests were at stake. Israel is this country's most dependable ally in a region that is vital to the economic well-being of the world. During the Cold War, Israel was a steadfast ally in a region containing many states that leaned toward the Soviet Union. In recent years, Israel has been an important exemplar of the merits of democracy and free markets.

Renewed war in the region carries high costs. It would threaten an important ally, demand materiel and financial support for that ally from the United States, and, not least, threaten the supply of petroleum to the developed world. Rogue regimes such as the governments of Iran, Iraq, and Libya would exploit the crisis to advance their agendas and destabilize other important allies in the region, including Egypt, Jordan, Saudi Arabia, and even Turkey.

Furthermore, the absence of a just peace in the region, one that restores opportunity to the Palestinian people, is a likely goad to further instability, including the terrorism that has marked the tactics of all players in this region at one point or another. In recent years, Americans have begun to perceive such terrorism as a direct threat to them, and its elimination or reduction was and is viewed as another important goal of the peace process.

In the preparation of this book, many of the senior officials of the U.S. government who were involved in the supervision of the Middle East Peace Initiative—and particularly in the development and execution of the economic elements of that initiative—were interviewed. These interviews came on the heels of the process of collecting similar information from their counterparts in the U.S. government who were responsible for the Haiti initiative. With the exception of one or two people who were actively involved in both initiatives, most had never met. Yet, the juxtaposition of the two initiatives had a striking effect, revealing similarities at every level, similarities that produced an economic peacekeeping effort in the Middle East that has been, by almost any measure, an enormous disappointment and was categorized by many familiar with it as having been—to date—a failure.

Common Objectives, Shared Pressures

The Middle East had suffered through years of warfare and terrorism and a legacy of ancient enmities. Haiti had simply suffered. The peace process in the Middle East involved many different countries—even the immediate, more narrow issue of the Palestinian Territories involved several entities, most notably Israel and Jordan. Haiti's problems were its own. Haiti had no tradition of economic or trading success. The Palestinians and the Israelis had a considerable tradition in this regard, one stretching back millennia to Gaza's days as one of the trading capitals of the ancient Holy Land.

Yet for the United States the goals of peace and stability were the same in both places and were declared to be a U.S. foreign policy priority by President Clinton. The Administration did not wish to ensure its goals with troops. It hoped that a combination of diplomacy and focused economic development efforts would give both regions a new chance.

In both regions, the stakes were high. The Clinton Administration had precious few foreign policy successes to point to, and for a considerable time it indeed looked as if its efforts in the Middle East and Haiti were to be its sole victories abroad. Consequently, within the Administration, the pressure was extremely great to ensure that these victories remained intact, and that the peaceful solutions to regional problems with which the United States was associated maintained popular support within the countries that we were trying to help. Furthermore, both initiatives were in large part undertaken as a consequence of pressure from special interest groups that were very important in American politics: African-Americans and Floridians in the case of Haiti, Jewish Americans and Arab-Americans in the case of the Middle East. These groups would scrutinize the Administration's efforts and demand that certain aspects of each situation be handled extremely carefully.

In order to maintain peaceful situations that had been created only recently and were still widely regarded as fragile, U.S. policy-makers focusing on Haiti and the Middle East ultimately saw that economic growth in these areas would be essential. Haitians and Palestinians alike had suffered enormously during the decades immediately preceding this one. Palestinians now had a standard of living that was a fraction of that of their Israeli neighbors. Haitians had the lowest standard of living in the Western Hemisphere. In both regions, the enemies of peace played upon the suffering and poverty of these people.

If Aristide's government did not produce growth—and in particular new jobs—it was considered highly likely that Haiti's fragile new democracy would be threatened by demagogues who would denounce the new way as being unsuccessful and bad for the average Haitian. In the same way, it was expected that opposition Palestinian groups, such as Hamas—which had opposed the more moderate path adopted by Fatah and its leader, Arafat, as well as the other Palestinian political entities that had signed on with Arafat—would continue to use the frustrations of Palestinians living as second-class citizens in their own homeland to fuel insurrection and undermine peace. Only if the new paths chosen by these peoples could be shown to create new economic and other opportunities could the opponents of peace and stability be reliably silenced.

Economic Planning Comes Second Again

Given these similarities and given the fact that the efforts to maintain peace were taking place within the same Administration—indeed they often were directed at the highest level in meetings that would take place consecutively in the same room chaired by the same people—it is not surprising that the two efforts would share many attributes. What is surprising, however, is that the attributes they shared were mostly negative—a lack of coordination and a lack of experience in dealing with the imperatives of emergency economics. According to senior officials, these negative characteristics manifested themselves first in the fact that in both cases the Administration conceived the original initiatives without real consideration of the economic issues involved.

It was only after Aristide was restored to Haiti and Arafat had signed the Accords on the White House lawn that any real effort was made within the U.S. government to address the demands of stimulating growth in those devastated, institutionless, poverty-stricken lands—demands far greater than Washington could meet in the way of resources. To be sure, meetings had taken place at the multilateral level some time before these watershed events, and within weeks of the dramatic ceremonies, the multilateral community was ready to begin some kind of work. In both cases, however, this economic planning was conducted by rote out of the old economic development playbook and without any careful consideration of the political objectives that were driving U.S. interests.

More Bandaids from AID

Because of limited resources for both the Haiti and Middle East initiatives, economic peacekeepers were forced to use very limited tools—essentially the existing programs of a few agencies of the U.S. government—tools that had not been designed for emergency situations and that were incapable of inducing the substantial infusions of capital and technical expertise needed to ensure success.

AID was at the core of both initiatives, and in both cases it earned the deep disdain of officials from other agencies with which it dealt. AID distinguished itself by its bureaucratic slowness, its resolute commitment

39

to procedures that were not working, its reflexive dependency on NGOs that had very little concern for the overarching policy goals of the U.S. government, its occasional incompetence, and its consistent unwillingness to adapt to the consensus of the rest of the Administration.

When, in the wake of the September 1993 signings, the President announced the U.S. government's financial commitment to peace in the Middle East, he spoke of a $500-million program over five years. AID would provide $375 million, while $125 million would come from OPIC. More than three years later, because OPIC is precisely the wrong tool to use—given that it uses a commercial standard to evaluate investments rather than the more relaxed standards required in such emergency situations—OPIC had approved precisely two projects in Gaza and the West Bank totaling less than $4 million dollars (a performance as underwhelming as that of OPIC's activity in Haiti).

Other agencies, such as the Export-Import Bank, were similarly precluded from being helpful in either situation. The Commerce Department could fly in planes full of business people but could do precious little more to induce the U.S. business community to invest. Having said that, it is clear that more attention needs to be paid to the interconnection between aid and trade policies. Individually incorporated enterprise funds could be very helpful and special insurance programs that give business people incentives to undertake heightened risks (see Conclusion 5, pp. 85-87) might also be of value, as would a greater willingness on the part of the USTR to offer access to U.S. markets more freely to struggling countries in which we have a defined national security interest. (Given the current mood regarding trade in Washington, officials are leery of risking other initiatives in the horse-trading that would inevitably result from such special pleading.)

While complaints about the international economic effort for the Middle East were reaching a crescendo outside the U.S. government, complaints about the U.S. effort were peaking internally. As in the Haiti case, these complaints initially focused on the work being done by AID, the primary U.S. aid distribution agency. Senior officials from throughout the government with whom we spoke cited malfunctioning bureaucratic snafus, intransigence on the setting of priorities, and insensitivity to the key political issues that the United States was supposed to be supporting. In one specific case, AID responded to Palestinian needs for improved drainage by, in the words of a senior State Department official, "putting in some pipes, pointing them all in one direction and creating a giant lake of sewage. They never once stopped to think about the effect the lake was having on the people who had to live along its 'banks'."

Prior to 1994, AID had resisted providing funds for recurring costs like police salaries and insisted that "institution building" and "long-term development" were more important. But, after a forced reorganization that left "a lot of blood on the floor," AID became much more responsive to projects that produced rapid employment and left tangible results. They also redressed past errors including draining the lake of sewage.

It should be said here that, given the structure of the U.S. government, AID is seen by all as absolutely crucial to U.S. emergency economic interventions. Its continuing reassessment of its role and the commitment of its leadership to improved results has shown significant positive results in all three cases studied. But it is also seen as an uneven agency with alternating pools of talent and shoals of bureaucracy. In an ideal world, reliance on AID might be replaced by a system that puts resources directly into the hands of the State Department regional bureaus with lead responsibility for individual crises or, better still, in the hands of a Treasury or White House team with special authority over emergency economic measures. (State is notoriously risk-averse; these situations often require bolder leadership that would have to come from a source closer to the political center of power in the bureaucracy.) Furthermore, in the turf-conscious environment in Washington, the more agencies become involved, the more delays and conflicts inevitably result. Consequently, where time or efficiency is of the essence—as in the emergency intervention here discussed—cutting out "middle men agencies" is desirable even in the best of cases (see recommendation for inter-agency economic rapid-response capability, Conclusion 1, p. 27).

A final note on AID: Some serious problems still remain. In reinventing itself, the organization actually may have thrown out some of the good with the bad. For example, AID backed away from funding indigenous Palestinian NGOs, heeding the often valid criticism that in many post-conflict situations, NGO support provides little immediate political benefit. However, in the Territories, the NGOs play a somewhat different role. Given the other constraints on economic progress—such as the border closings and the problems within the PA—funding those hundreds of NGOs would likely help undermine Hamas, which provides the majority of social services to the Palestinians (and which is itself the recipient of millions of dollars in aid from nations around the region that wish to undermine the peace process and support Islamic fundamentalism). In emergency economic interventions, as in other aspects of foreign policy, taking a case-by-case approach is critical; while academics or pundits may crave consistency, policy-makers should not be slaves to formulas born of other realities or devised to serve other ends.

The problems with the Middle East economic initiative that were caused by the limitations and deficiencies of various U.S. government agencies were compounded by the lack of a central coordinating mechanism. Such a mechanism was discussed but never came to pass. Mid-level discussions took place among agencies. The Commerce Department led missions, funded and staffed a U.S.–Israel Science and Technology Commission, and promoted a list of projects open for investment at the business summits that took place in Casablanca and Amman. The State Department's economic team played a lead role in coordinating those summits. Other agencies worked at the margins. Ironically, and illuminatingly, all this ad hoc activity was going on precisely when the U.S. government recognized and acted upon the need for a coordinated, centralized initiative in Haiti. This particular realization did not, however, make it down the right corridors or into the right conference rooms to influence a similar process with a similar problem in the Middle East.

BOSNIA

In Bosnia, the stated mission was similar to the two cases discussed above. The President of the United States had decided that it was a foreign policy priority to promote peace and stability in a nation beyond our shores. At the same time, domestic politics demanded an exit strategy. Consequently, the Administration felt that a combination of limited military involvement, aggressive diplomacy, and focused economic development efforts was the means by which the U.S. could accomplish our objectives and offer new hope to a region victimized by conflict.

The Dayton Accords came just a year before the 1996 U.S. elections. Bosnia was a high-risk situation. Peace could only be achieved through the deployment of U.S. troops and thus the exposure of tens of thousands of Americans to significant danger. Furthermore, Haiti, the Middle East, and Bosnia had come to be seen as among the foremost foreign policy achievements of the Clinton Administration. In an election year, a slip in any one would soon be fodder for the opposition.

In the General Framework for Peace struck at Wright Patterson Air Force Base in Dayton, Ohio, economic issues were high on the list of negotiators' concerns. "Without economic reconstruction," said Richard Holbrooke, Dayton's key architect, "there cannot be peace in the region . . . There was never a moment that I did not believe that economic reconstruction was the key to bringing these ethnically warring tribes together."

No Consensus, Poor Coordination

Economic analysis necessarily includes consideration of military and political issues. Ambivalence about the crisis in Bosnia not only allowed it to fester but now threatens to undermine the peace that was postponed for so long. There is no consensus about the objective of the peace effort. Is it, as some Europeans and the Russians suggest, simply to bring an end to the fighting even if that means rewarding aggressors and soft-peddling their punishment? Is it, as some Americans and Islamic leaders suggest, to bring peace but also to punish aggressors, sending a message to them and to those who might think to emulate them elsewhere in the Balkans or in the wider world? Is it to enshrine in the policies of the Western alliance an idea of self-determination, giving any fairly homogeneous group of people the right to secede from any state? Or is it to support the ideal of the multi-ethnic state, fearful that making homogeneity a prerequisite for independence invites future onslaughts of "ethnic cleansing"? Or is it to embrace the Balkans as "Southeastern Europe"?

There is a variety of answers to these questions, yet the blunt reality is that neither the international community that has come together to address the problems of Bosnia nor the U.S. domestic political community speaks with a single voice. Goals, motives, and analyses are different. Levels of commitment to solving the problem are different. Consequently, U.S. and allied policy-makers have made a mistake with respect to the civilian side of the peace effort that the military would never have allowed with matters under its purview. The military went into Bosnia with a clear mission, a defined timeframe, and a phobia for "mission creep." Their tasks were limited and clearly tactical. On the civilian side, some of the objectives seem to be strategic and long-term, others short-term. Some policy-makers are thinking of the consequences for Europe, others for domestic politics in the United States; some are thinking of religious issues, others are contemplating nationalistic concerns. As a result, the reconstruction effort has been in precarious shape from the outset.

The price of these failures of public policy can be measured economically as well. The costs of supporting the one million refugees from the Bosnia War and the peacekeeping troops and of supplying humanitarian aid may total as much as $40-50 billion above and beyond the costs of reconstruction. A fraction of that money could have prevented the destruction in the first place.

Despite the belated recognition that coordination of the Haitian and Middle Eastern economic peacekeeping initiatives was essential, once again in the Bosnian case the U.S. government found itself without an effective coordinating mechanism. Progress nonetheless was made, but complaints were common about disorganization, the lack of shared objectives, and turf battles.

Once again, AID was cited as a bureaucratic logjam, an impediment to the achievement of short-term objectives, and an organization without any real understanding of the potential role that the private sector can and should play in such efforts. AID was responsible for the bulk of the assistance funds, and once again it was open to criticism that its culture—with its traditional biases toward guiding program development and its traditional NGO partners receiving much of the money—was not attuned to the demands of the situation. While AID's approach produced some progress in road building and in other areas, it did little to advance organic private sector growth or investment.

FILLING THE INSTITUTIONAL GAP

In the wake of the Gulf War, the military strategists of the world buzzed with the new jargon of "low-intensity" or "regional" conflict. Rapid deployment forces were conceived to cope with the realities posed by this new paradigm for warfare. In the wake of the Middle East peace efforts of the past few years, new paradigms in peacekeeping have emerged as well. Economic issues are beginning to be recognized as central to the hopes of embattled peoples and consequently to the hopes for peace. At the same time, old development models, even economic peacekeeping models dating back just a few decades, are inapplicable and misleading. A new means for ensuring stability through creating immediate, highly visible, politically significant signs of economic development is needed: an economic rapid-response capability.

Such an economic rapid-response team should be led from the White House–based Office for International Economic Security Initiatives proposed earlier. The team should be interdisciplinary, interagency, and should include security specialists, political specialists, and military specialists (who can plan hand-offs from military to non-military agencies). The team should be involved in coordinating the economic dimension of all interventions, even if special task forces are created to handle individual intervention cases. It should control and plan the disposition of all funds earmarked for the interventions it is overseeing. It should have the capacity to direct the U.S. role in multilateral donor activities. The team should also have access to tools that can truly create incentives for private sector investment: insurance programs for high-risk situations, grant programs, and special high-risk enterprise funds in which it is clearly specified that achieving a political result is as important as generating a financial return. These are not programs that currently exist. They should be created and administered by the proposed rapid response team in conjunction with the relevant host agencies. The establishment of the Office of Transition Initiatives within AID is an improvement, but AID as currently configured is not the optimal organization to spearhead post-intervention economic efforts, given the major political exigencies that must be addressed.

To aid in the creation of the coordinating Office for International Economic Security Initiatives and the economic rapid-response team, funding resources within the foreign policy apparatus need to be strengthened. The State Department needs the wherewithal to ensure that U.S. embassies worldwide have the right balance between political/military personnel and economic personnel. In peacetime situations, adding economic personnel makes sense, given the increasing importance of economic relations to our foreign policy. In post-intervention situations such as that in Haiti, having additional resources in the embassy to monitor and manage economic efforts is essential. Furthermore, whatever intelligence apparatus is being relied on by policy-makers in Washington or elsewhere must become better tuned to identifying the key economic issues and players and tracking developments on the economic front.

CONCLUSION 2: MASTER THE LOCAL POLITICS OF EMERGENCY ECONOMICS

"You can't build an economic house on a political sinkhole." To determine the nature of the ground on which it is attempting to build, the U.S. government must realistically appraise the local political and military situation. It should also assess whether local public and private sector partners in an affected region share our goals, and, if they do not, whether there are effective alternatives to achieve those goals. Conditionality is key.

Perhaps the greatest problem of all for economic peacekeepers lies in this fact: Even the best of plans for economic intervention in behalf of peace and stability cannot work if the political and security preconditions for peace are not in place. Bosnia is the obvious example, although certainly recent events in the Middle East support this point as well. If in a situation like Bosnia fundamental questions remain unanswered about the international community's or the local leaders' objectives, if fundamental strategic issues remain divisive, and if fundamental security and political matters have not been resolved, then the economic intervention is compromised from the outset. Similarly, if a plan is put into place but efforts are not made to ensure its political success—free and fair elections, for example—then economic efforts to support the plan will prove inadequate or futile. Economic intervention is a vitally important component of peacekeeping, but the fighting must stop first.

In Haiti, the Middle East, and Bosnia, U.S. reconstruction efforts have been stymied in many cases by the very governments or entities we are trying to help. Thus policy-makers need to better analyze and understand the objectives of our local "partners" in these efforts. In addition, once aid efforts are under way, the United States must insist on strict conditionality for our help. It is essential that all parties to reconstruction activity know from the outset that aid efforts of every sort (financial, political, military, and technical) are to be based on adherence to narrowly drawn and focused principles and terms agreed in advance, and that the plug will be pulled if these are violated. Washington must be willing to distance itself from its allies or the recipients of aid if they do not adhere to the terms of the going-in agreements. Failure to stand tough promotes the perception that the U.S. needs those we are helping more than they need us.

Local government and domestic interest groups can lay waste to international economic reconstruction efforts. Central to the planning process, therefore, must be an assessment of the strengths, weaknesses, and difficulties presented by local partners and other factions on the ground. In addition, we must consistently maintain and build local political support for our objectives, or our assistance is not going to be effective. We must recognize, going in, that some factors will remain outside U.S. control—a case for both rigorous, continuing analysis and occasional acceptance of less than 100 percent success. We must also direct our efforts where they will do the most good, which again requires constant planning and re-assessment. In these situations, all economics is political as well as local.

AN INSCRUTABLE STALL IN HAITI

"What happened?" former U.S. Ambassador to Haiti Ernest Preeg suggests the people of Haiti asked as promises of economic revitalization went unfulfilled. The real question is: "What didn't happen?" The answer, put simply, is: "Privatization." While privatization was by no means the only challenge facing the Haitian government, it became the line in the sand on the economic battleground.

The only way to truly address Haiti's power problems was through the privatization and professional management of Electricité d'Haiti. Both were necessary because it was only through privatization that the needed investment flows could be generated. A management contract, while a useful temporary fix, would very quickly be found to be insufficient. Privatization was similarly needed to improve the other basic infrastructure elements of the Haitian economy: the ports, the airport, the telephone company. In addition, it was clear that the Haitian government had more problems than it had qualified staff to handle. Offloading the parastatals to professional managers with an equity interest in the future of these companies was essential if the problems were to be addressed. Finally, privatization would take these severely wounded companies off the books of the government and would offer, instead of liabilities, real cash that the government itself could determine how to invest. This was a clear winner across the board, and many at the highest levels of the Haitian government—especially Prime Minister Smarck Michel, Finance Minister Marie-Michelle Rey, Presidential Chief of Staff Leslie Voltaire, and Central Bank Governor Leslie Delatour—acknowledged as much.

But privatization, even when called "democratization" by the Aristide government, was opposed by the nationalists in Lavalas, the President's party, as a giveaway of national assets. When President Clinton went to Haiti to oversee the transfer of command of the multinational ground troops to the United Nations, banners in the crowd accused

Michel, Rey, and others of plotting against Aristide by supporting privatization.

Later, once the results of the International Finance Corporation (IFC) privatization study were nearly ready and the bidding process was to be unveiled, internecine fighting broke out within the Aristide government. Michel and Rey were under attack from another group of ministers led by Planning Minister Jean Marie Cherestal. Pamphlets attacking them were distributed by people getting out of cars with government license plates. President Aristide himself tried to appear above it all, and when that was impossible, tried to take both sides—assuring U.S. officials that privatization was a top priority while placating opponents with his clear ambivalence. Behind the scenes, however, he worked against reform—a fact that became openly obvious during 1997, when he split with Préval over reforms, forcing the resignation of Prime Minister Smarth.

Privatization was, however, so central to real progress on economic reform that the international community, led by the U.S., adopted it as a precondition for the IMF Structural Adjustment Credit (SAC) agreement that was required if the government of Haiti was to receive the donor funds that constituted almost half of its fiscal 1996 budget. The timing could not have been worse. The 1996 fiscal year began in October. The SAC was needed before then. Progress on privatization was needed before that. And, in Haiti, the run-up to the December presidential elections had begun even as a newly elected parliament prepared to meet for the very first time in mid-October. Aristide—still sending mixed signals about his own intention to run—talked progress and then did not move forward. He promised concrete actions and then fought against taking those actions. Ultimately, Michel and Rey left the government as a consequence of this impasse, and the new Prime Minister's platform was essentially "do nothing until the elections."

The Clinton Administration had launched a plan that depended entirely on the cooperation of an undependable ally for long-term success. Some have suggested that President Aristide would have been more committed to making economic progress and less concerned about special interest groups within his party were he not forced to contend with the December presidential elections and four years as a power behind the throne. These observers believe that if he had been able to serve out his term, he would have felt accountable to the Haitian people and compelled to provide real results. As it turned out, Aristide was able to leave the tough decisions on the economy to Préval, who has considerably less popular support than Aristide. To his credit, Préval so far has taken on the tough issues and produced significantly more progress than his more celebrated predecessor.

It is difficult to imagine the United States providing more resources than it did to help the Haitians. Yet, without cooperation from those we were trying to help, such mobilization was undermined and in some cases mooted. Part of the non-cooperation came from internal problems beyond the control of the Haitians, such as lack of infrastructure. Part of the problem was a result of conflicts of will. In some cases, the problem was exacerbated by conflicting messages emanating from the presidential palace.

The fundamental failure of the Haitian government to rise to the economic challenge before it, and the active efforts of its leader to oppose U.S. economic objectives, suggest a potentially fatal and certainly dangerous primary flaw within U.S. policy toward post-intervention regions: Motivated by a potent mixture of politics and ideals, the U.S. government fails to recognize or accept its own limitations in carrying out its policies.

Surely the United States cannot dispute the right of the Haitians to pursue their own course. Assuring them of their ability to exercise that right via the mechanisms of democracy was, after all, the primary reason the United States said it was in Haiti. However, the fact remains that the United States mounted a costly and controversial foreign policy initiative and found that in many crucial respects the eventual outcome was out of Washington's hands. This is a problem with which would-be nation-builders have suffered as long as they have been around. To evaluate the likely success of the civilian side of virtually all international initiatives, U.S. policy-makers also must accept that our power to influence events is greatly limited—especially if budgets are contracting and particularly when we are unwilling to be as aggressive as we might be with conditionality on our aid.

Having recognized this, we should make an assessment, acknowledging that the flip side of the argument about our limitations is the reality that something less than 100 percent success is often good enough in an imperfect world—but only if a less than perfect outcome is what we have set our expectations for at the outset. (In the case of Haiti, good enough would be anything beyond the minimum required to keep Haitian boat people off the high seas and heading for Florida.)

DÉJÀ VU IN THE MIDDLE EAST

Substitute the name Arafat for Aristide, and you get the same kinds of complaints from officials. Both new regimes lacked the experience and the bureaucratic depth to administer important programs. Both were hotbeds of corruption and incompetence. Both leaders were linked to special interest groups in their respective countries. Both regimes were internally divided and offered the ridiculous spectacle of senior officials simultaneously announcing or advocating completely different points of view or actions. Both failed to live up to budget projections and channeled dollars that could have gone to important project work into balance-of-payments support. And perhaps most disturbing, both actively resisted key elements of the economic recovery programs that were clearly in their best interests.

In the Middle East case, the frustrations in no way were limited to the Palestinian authorities. Indeed, viewed exclusively from an economic recovery perspective, by far the most destructive single act taken by any authority was the Israeli government's decision to close its borders after each terrorist incident in the country. These interdictions, particularly those that took place in the wake of the 1996 bombings, have had a crushing impact on that significant percentage of the Palestinian workforce that depends on traveling to Israel to earn a living.

In both cases, local politics has been a bane of the economic peace process. The election campaign and Aristide's perception of his own political needs forced him to back away from key reforms. Israeli politics have kept the borders shut more often than open, and the election of Benjamin Netanyahu as Prime Minister temporarily stalled the peace process overall as both sides waited to evaluate the consequences of the new, harder-line Israeli leadership. At the same time, political fragility in both Haiti and the Palestinian Territories has kept business people and investors away, waiting and watching, uncertain about the next changes and their consequences for regional stability. The result has been a weakening of support for the changes that had been so actively backed by the U.S. government. That is not to say that failure is imminent in either case. The net effect of the economic initiatives undertaken in these countries is still unclear, although it is equally fair to speculate that, without the steps that have been taken, the situations in either region would be considerably less comfortable today.

The United States miscalculated on some key economic costs that would ensue from the implementation of the Oslo accords. To cite some examples, the costs of maintaining the Palestinian police force ballooned from 9,000 men in initial estimates to more than double that today, and predictions that the responsibility for tax collection could be transferred from the Israeli government to the Palestinian Authority (which would suddenly develop an aptitude for the task) proved absurdly optimistic. Provisions in the Economic Protocol signed in 1994 called for some lost tax revenues to be transfered from the Israelis back to the Palestinian Authority, but these covered only a fraction of the amount that was needed to meet original assumptions. (This was in large part due to inaccurate assumptions about the speed with which Israeli forces would actually be withdrawn from the West Bank and elections held.)

In addition, the assumptions behind Palestinian economic projections did not include expectations of prolonged and costly border closings. The World Bank estimates that in 1996 alone, such closings cost the Palestinian economy some $957 million. What is more, in response to the instability caused by these closings, Israeli businesses have taken a variety of measures that threaten to do permanent damage. Over 20,000 jobs that once went to Palestinians have been eliminated, and a like number have been given to Thais and others who have been flown in as replacement workers. Gaza's GDP has now fallen to half of its 1987 level. In the words of Gaza specialist and critic of Israel Sarah Roy, "Israeli security is far more threatened by a hungry, frustrated population on its borders than by open borders that would allow that population to live a decent, normal life. When that happens, terrorism will stop." While this analysis is easily assailable from the perspective of those concerned with Israeli security (who would argue that borders will open when terrorism does stop), the consequences of the closings are clear to observers of every political stripe, and they have been devastating.

The full impact of such closings is understood when their cost is measured against the outlays that have, in fact, been made by the international donor community. Those outlays have been very slow. As of late 1997, total pledges were approximately $3.6 billion. Of that, firm commitments added up to $3 billion. Actual disbursements totaled only just over $1.8 billion. Many observers believe that border closures have cost the Palestinians significantly more than that amount. Yasir Arafat himself said—at the 1996 World Economic Forum annual meeting in Davos—that such closures had cost more than "all the pledges of aid we have received." (The World Bank has estimated that in 1994-96, the border closure cost to the Palestinian economy was approximately $2.8 billion, or roughly double the $1.49 billion in donor fund disbursements during the same period.)

Finally, one of the problems cited by many critics of the multilateral effort was its unwillingness to set conditions with teeth to ensure compliance with multilateral objectives. While multilateral efforts are not the focus of this study, the U.S. government, if it is to be dependent on such efforts to implement its own policies, must recognize from both the Haiti and the Middle East experiences that *strict conditionality from the outset* is the only way to motivate reluctant, sometimes inchoate or otherwise organizationally challenged entities on the ground.

Israel and the Palestinians: Partnership for Progress?

One organizationally challenged entity was the Palestinian Authority (PA). As in the Haiti situation, the economic component of U.S. peacekeeping efforts in the Territories was retarded by conflicts and problems with our local "partner," the entity that we were ostensibly trying to assist. (In the interest of fairness, it should again be pointed out that the Israelis also played a crucial role in undermining initial assumptions and making the economic reconstruction task more difficult. Examples concerning Israel follow the section on the Palestinian Authority.)

Wasta is the Arab word for influence. In any new government, the competition for such influence shapes the entity and defines those who hold real power. In a government comprised primarily of former revolutionaries with little administrative experience, such a competition might be expected to be sometimes divisive and a factor compounding the other difficulties in getting the new institutional structure to operate properly. The PA in its earliest days lived down to such expectations— and indeed illustrated them for future graduate school case studies. In one instance, two competing ministries simultaneously announced two different outcomes to a hotly contested telecommunications deal—presumably as a consequence of special arrangements that had been made with each. This confusion was a direct result of the fact that the PA was the successor to the Palestine Liberation Organization (PLO), and the PLO had roots in Palestine and an operational headquarters in Tunis. For a while, the two Palestinian centers operated with minimal coordination and often with a total lack thereof.

Problems Within the Palestinian Authority

Soon, three separate bodies were given responsibility for managing the economic development process of the new entity. These included PEC-DAR, the Palestinian Economic Council for Development and Reconstruction, which was created to provide a liaison with multilateral donors; the Ministry of Finance; and the Ministry of Planning and International Cooperation—all three of which were initially in a heightened state of turf warfare. As in many other places in the world, some saw *wasta* as a ticket to profit, and allegations of influence peddling, bribery, the solicitation of "commissions," and other such behaviors have been common. Furthermore, the centrality of Arafat to the process also served to give his office a chop on most major decisions and consequently opened the way for more infighting and confusion.

These problems led directly to a reluctance on the part of all donors, including the United States, to move forward with programs for which the PA could not demonstrate that funds would be allocated, "absorbed," and distributed wisely or even moderately efficiently. This contributed in part to the slowdown in dissemination of funds that was cited earlier. In addition, the budget problems noted above have prompted a series of efforts to gain a commitment to fiscal responsibility

53

from Arafat and his cabinet. An early 1997 agreement sought a budget surplus within two years. At the same time, much as in Haiti, donors are not entirely sure that the numbers they are getting are reliable (this despite mandated periodic audits), and there are concerns, cited by McGill University's Rex Brynen, that there may be a "shadow budget" operating beyond the knowledge of aid officials.

The distinguished Swiss newspaper *Neue Zuercher Zeitung* wrote in February 1997:

> Arafat's unsupervised and self-interested use of aid funds, his financial contacts to offshore financial centers and his ties to murky speculators, arms merchants and financial hustlers—all this does not bode well for the future. In the face of all the accusations of corruption and political patronage with public funds, this Nobel Prize winner consistently resists orderly record-keeping and turns a deaf ear to calls for external financial oversight.

> As a result, Arafat's image is not much better in business circles than it is among his political opponents. There are strong doubts as to whether he will keep his promises about investment guarantees, land and tax concessions. Talks in the corridors of the recent Arab-Israeli summit in Amman revealed that businessmen are mainly inclined to consider projects that are as far removed as possible from the grasp of the PA in Jericho.

Israel and the Paradox of Economic Self-Defense

The great underlying economic challenge of peace is that it depends on a Palestinian autonomy that is, at least at the moment, an economic impossibility. As noted in regard to border closings—by far the most economically destabilizing action taken by any party to the peace process—the Palestinian Territories are highly dependent on Israel for economic growth. Israel's $65-billion economy is the potential locomotive to pull the train of Palestinian development. The customs union called for in the Economic Protocol gives the Palestinians access to an important "export" market and makes the Territories tempting manufacturing locations for businesses interested in the Israeli market. That said, the customs union also gives the greatest advantage to Israeli investors seeking to capitalize on the cheap manufacturing possibilities of the Territories and takes away a significant potential revenue source from the Palestinians—tariffs, which, although politically incorrect, remain one of the most easily collected revenue sources for a new government.

As *The Economist* reported,

> For many, life is even harder than it used to be. In part, that is the PA's fault: exasperated foreign donors point to corruption within it,

and to Mr. Arafat's determination to keep hold of its purse strings. A bigger reason is the way Israel puts into practice its zeal for security.

In the past, a Palestinian businessman might drive from Gaza via Israel and the occupied West Bank to Amman in Jordan in five or six hours. Now, because of Israeli searches and insistence on an Israeli escort, it can take up to 18 hours. Palestinian lorries on the trip have to go in convoy, and are subject to complex paperwork and intricate searches—the kind that can ruin a refrigerated load—that may mean a week on the road. Palestinian imports and exports through Israeli ports and airports must be carried, when in Israel, by Israeli lorries. This means slow and costly transfers between vehicles. . .

The result is that exports of Palestinian fruit and vegetables rot in the sun; machinery imports are mysteriously delayed; and would-be Palestinian entrepreneurs have to engage Israeli middle-men (who may well . . . deliberately give inferior service). (*The Economist*, February 10, 1996.)

Reports of problems with Israeli red tape or arrangements favoring Israeli businessmen over their Palestinian counterparts are legion. One infamous case involved the repeated, lengthy, and often inexplicable delays in simply getting phone lines installed at PECDAR, allegedly an entity in support of the peace process, an Israeli interest. Other anecdotes tell of Palestinian importers seeking required permissions from Israeli authorities only to have them delayed long enough for Israeli competitors to seize the advantage.

It is inarguable that both governments are being shortsighted in impeding sustainable economic growth for the Palestinian people. But both are run by politicians, and it is equally inarguable that politics, being rooted in the moment, is by nature short-sighted. Thus, particularly in inchoate democracies like the Palestinian Territories and Haiti, as well as in established democracies such as Israel, the United States and other donors must recognize that emergency economic assistance, like peace itself, is a *political* game. We must maintain or build political support for our objectives or our assistance is not going to be effective, even if the plans for it have been lifted directly out of the pages of the best economic textbook. Our great challenge is to build the needed political support while working within the constraints of the local political situation and institutions of the target region and within the constraints of our own political will.

By 1994, the United States and most other donors involved in the Middle East peace process realized that, as in Haiti, visible economic results of political significance were needed—and fast. As in Haiti, the greatest obstacles we faced were the policies of our partner governments and the political situation on the ground, which were beyond our power to control. The United States and other donor governments must recognize that the political force we intend to deliver with our economic actions must be carefully directed to effectively impact on not only the opponents of peace but also the policies of our friends.

It's Not Just the Economy

Even if the United States had followed all of the above recommendations, it would not have saved the economic recovery initiative in the Middle East, although the initiative would have been more effective. A nation's security is a lot like that of its leaders. It is impossible to protect a government official against the attack of a dedicated assassin who is willing to give up his or her own life or freedom. Similarly, if within any country a group exists that is committed to disrupting a peace process, and if it is well enough funded and sufficiently dedicated, it can subvert and disrupt.

The assassination of Prime Minister Rabin, the terror bombings of Israeli citizens, and the linkage between these events and the election of Prime Minister Netanyahu illustrate that, especially in volatile settings such as the Middle East, even a handful of opponents can derail a process and undo much progress. The suicide bombings of late February and early March 1996 resulted in the closing of Israeli borders to Palestinians, higher Palestinian unemployment, their greater economic pain, and consequently greater opportunity for opponents of the peace process. Once begun, a vicious circle is hard to break.

All Economics Is Local

Economic development is just one vector of force that we can bring to bear to influence events in the direction of U.S. national interests. Development should neither be over- nor under-estimated. The disruptions that have paralyzed the process of economic growth in the Palestinian Territories serve to illustrate the need for other tools, including support for tighter security and diplomatic pressure. At the same time, the pervasive nature of economic need often works in ways that make it hard to evaluate results. Has the creation of jobs undermined Hamas recruitment? Has improvement of the quality of life won additional support for the PA? Has the example of Israeli development suggested to Palestinians that it is time to stop fighting and start building?

An article in an Israeli magazine, The Jerusalem Report (June 27, 1996), illustrates the power of economic persuasion very well by offering evidence that the suicide bombings and the Israeli reaction to them might be having exactly the opposite effect of that intended by the bombers:

"The situation was bad before the arrival of the Palestinian Authority and it's got worse since," says Eyad Dabadish, of the Shati
refugee camp, as he idles away the afternoon with a few similarly
unemployed neighbors, a toddler on his lap. "Under Israeli rule,
we lived better."

Sabi'a Baker, a father of five in his 30s, concedes that the constant tension and violence of the days of the Intifada have dissi-
pated. "OK, there's no fear," he says, "But there's no food either.
How do you expect a man like me, young, with kids, without one
shekel in my pocket, to feel about this peace?"

He asks only for the border with Israel to be opened up. "We
want to live with the Israelis, as one people," he says.

It's a common theme. One taxi driver talks nostalgically about
the early 1980s, before the Intifada, when Menachem Begin was
Prime Minister and hard-liner Ariel Sharon was Minister of
Defense. "Then, everything was open to us," he reminisces, "there
were no borders."

Elsewhere in the same issue, the magazine suggests economic reasons why Netanyahu is likely to continue to support the peace process:

A move away from the peace process will affect Israel's international standing and jeopardize the trade links Israel has developed
in countries like Malaysia, Indonesia, Vietnam and China. Economic prosperity here depends on one thing: exports. You need
relations with as many markets as possible to make investments
here work. A return to a xenophobic Israel would be an economic disaster.

[Another] reason that he will continue along the Oslo path is
that he needs the closure to minimize the security risks to Israel.
On the other hand, he knows he cannot create a time-bomb on
the other side of the pre-67 border. He has to therefore foster
international investment in the Territories so that the jobs lost to
Palestinians in Israel will be created there. The Oslo framework is
the conduit to this happening.

The setbacks of late 1996 and early 1997 have demonstrated the
underlying truth behind these conclusions. However uncomfortable
Netanyahu and the Likud seem to be with Arafat and the Palestinians—
namely, regarding the Hebron stand-off and solution—they find that
deal they must. This is not to say that progress is inexorable; rather, it is
to appreciate that the pressures to sustain it are great.

57

BITING THE HAND THAT FEEDS
IN BOSNIA

If in Haiti and the Middle East the "beneficiary" governments of Aristide and Arafat turned out to be among the greatest impediments to economic recovery, the problem was compounded in Bosnia, where the problems were exacerbated by the fact that the predecessor governments were socialist states that had yet to accept or develop working market models. Furthermore, corruption was perhaps even more widespread than it had been in Haiti or the Middle East, with the cronies of nationalists in each camp—Serb, Muslim, and Croat—controlling key industries and eager to maintain that control as aid flows once again put riches within their grasp. Finally, these local governments were only partially implementing the other elements of the Dayton Peace Accords—with regard to freedom of movement, for example, and fair elections—thus adding an element of tension that complicated economic work in areas controlled by each.

One anecdote that emerged from Bosnia illustrates how intractable local leaders can sabotage a reconstruction effort. The mayor of a Bosnian town was noted for his refusal to comply with the civilian requirements of the Dayton Peace Accords, especially the imperative that refugees be allowed to return to their homes. He was offered the construction of a power plant, a project that would have provided good jobs for hundreds of households in his constituency. His response was, "I cannot be bought." For economic aid to have a positive impact on the political climate in Bosnia and in similar situations, ways must be found to co-opt or to force compliance from local leaders, or we will get nowhere.

Asked about the prospects for a multi-ethnic state, one Serbian leader derisively described Serbs and Muslims as "cats and dogs" and suggested that it would be absolutely unnatural for the two to mix. This, of course, was post-Dayton, and the comment came from one of those charged by the Dayton Accords with overseeing the creation of the multi-ethnic federation that Bosnia-Herzegovina was to become.

As Jane Perlez wrote in the *New York Times:*

> Though the Dayton Peace Accords have stopped the military conflict, the leaders of Bosnia, Serbia and Croatia have refused to loosen their grip on the economies that gave each of them a power base during the war, say Western economists, business leaders and government officials . . . By perpetuating their fiefs built on spoils and patronage, the politicians are obstructing economic changes—and development of entrepreneurs and regional markets—that could help dilute the virulent nationalism that propelled the contest. . . .

Foreign investment has failed to materialize because Western companies and financial institutions are leery of sinking money into bankrupt state-run agencies . . . In general, Western financial assistance to Bosnia has been far lower than was envisioned immediately after the Dayton Accords, but donor countries were dissuaded by the fact that the Government remained in firm control of the economy and there were no signs of imminent privatization. (*The New York Times*, August 20, 1996.)

Perlez also noted that in Serbia, Bosnia, and Croatia, cronies, party members, and others close to the leadership are enriching themselves while impeding reform. Croatian President Franjo Tudjman's party members are often favored in privatization results. Throughout the region, financing and licensing are controlled by profiteers close to the political elites. In Bosnia, the heads of key government agencies are from President Alija Izetbegovic's Party of Democratic Action. His close associates, like the close associates of Serb and Croat leaders, also run the media. They have resisted or blocked efforts to create independent television stations financed by the West and thus clearly have set back reforms on several levels.

Jonathan Landay of the *Christian Science Monitor,* writing in the *Washington Quarterly*, has similarly argued:

. . . the Achilles Heel of the Dayton Accords [is that] they institutionalize and strengthen the power of Bosnia's nationalist parties and their communist-style bureaucracies and militaries and do little to nurture a rebirth of the war-shattered moderate political middle ground. . . .

Dayton's boosters contend that internationally funded reconstruction and economic reintegration will bolster peace. I would argue the opposite is just as likely: Economic reconstruction without political reconstruction could further bolster the ruling nationalists. (*The Washington Quarterly*, Summer 1996.)

Landay recommended that the United States use its "considerable" economic leverage to force Dayton compliance by local leaders.

That leverage is overstated and has diminished rapidly since September 1996, when the national elections were given the stamp of legitimacy by the multilateral Organization for Security and Cooperation in Europe. With the political will to support the "follow-on" force in the region unclear and fragile, our military leverage in Bosnia is diminishing, although it is still considerable and crucial to maintaining the peace. With a split among the donors regarding conditionality, economic leverage is undercut as well. Meanwhile, the dollars continue to flow government to government, if not from the United States then from the Europeans or the Russians or the multilateral institutions, and, as they do, they strengthen the nationalist forces that must be weakened if Dayton is to have a chance at success. The United States—to its credit here—has been increasingly insistent on strict adherence to the conditions for funds disbursement that we set out in advance. While this has caused tensions between us and governments in Bosnia, it is a crucial source of leverage and credibility for our diplomatic and security efforts.

The obstacles presented by problems emanating from local "partners" on the ground were compounded in Bosnia by several even more fundamental elements stemming from the political/military situation. These were the scale of devastation wrought by the war, the continued presence in power of those who caused the war, and, most important, the lack of a definitive end to the war. None of these issues was effectively taken into account or dealt with prior to implementing economic reconstruction plans.

Neither the poverty of Haiti nor the squalor of Gaza presents an economic wasteland comparable to that produced by the fiercest land war in Europe in half a century. Virtually no family or town escaped unscathed. The human toll took many forms. The more than 300,000 casualties are just the tip of the iceberg. Some estimates suggest the number is 50 percent higher, and that perhaps 50,000 of the wounded were children. Behind each loss was unimaginable trauma. The indictments of Radovan Karadzic and General Ratko Mladic by the International War Crimes Tribunal cite genocide specifically. The mass murder of 8,000 men and boys near Srebrenica one hot summer day in 1995 was the worst such crime since the second World War. The men responsible remain at large, and there is serious question as to whether they will be brought to justice. This adds yet another element of trauma to the disruption and cost of making refugees of more than half of the population. The loss to Bosnia of one million people, including the vast majority of the region's intelligentsia, has multiple consequences for the future. Many are reluctant to return, awaiting signs that the peace will hold. And still others who remained now plan to leave.

In the words of a young man quoted in a *New York Times Magazine* piece on Bosnia's wounded younger generation:

"This is the Balkans," Nedim says, " . . . and this is a place where there will always be war. So maybe now it is O.K., but it will happen again. Because my grandfather was a refugee from war, then my father and then me. So I don't want my child to have a war, too. It is better to go and try to make some future in a place where this doesn't happen." "When that happens," he says, "then I will leave. I will take my family out of here, I will leave everything else, and I will say, "To hell with Bosnia, because I will not be a soldier anymore for them."

Ines has already picked out her preferred destination. "I want to go to America," she says, gazing out over the water. "One thing I like very much about America is that all the people there are so mixed. My feeling is that no one will ask me, "Are you a Croat, are you Muslim?" There it is safe because no one can find me." (Scott Anderson, "Bosnia's Last Best Hope," *New York Times Magazine*, September 8, 1996.)

It is no wonder that such attitudes prevail, but it is a grave threat to the future economic recovery of Bosnia, however the state is ultimately constituted.

Reform efforts also have been frustrated by the fact that the new governments of Serbia, Croatia, and Bosnia are run by the same men who waged and profited from the war. As a *U.S. News & World Report* article (August 26, 1996) on the importance of economic recovery to preserving peace indicated: "The threat of lower living standards obviously did nothing to prevent Yugoslavia's ethnic war in the first place." Indeed some republics felt economically exploited or short-changed which created animosities later fanned by opportunistic demagogues. Consequently, the goal must be to create an environment in which leaders stand to gain more from peace. In the case of Bosnia, efforts directed at leaders almost certainly also need to include those running the neighboring countries, Croatia and Serbia, who played such a critical role in the war and will continue to play a role in any permanent peace or resumption of war.

The jury is still out on how well the United States and the wider international aid effort have met the challenges and taken advantage of the opportunities in Bosnia. Two years after the signing of the Dayton Accords, the brutal war has not resumed. However, renewed outbreaks of violence between Muslims and Serbs in November 1996 and reports through 1997 of threats being used to prevent resettlement of war refugees illustrate how perilously fragile the peace is. Reconstruction efforts have so far done little to stabilize the situation. Various actors on all sides seem to be preparing for another outbreak of war by obstructing efforts to remove land mines, stockpiling weapons, or preventing the return of "alien" refugees. For too many Serbs, Croats, and Bosniaks, peace is not a consolidated fact that can be relied upon and that offers hope of a better life in the future.

U.S. planners must take a more strategic approach to the political implications of economic initiatives. It must become an element of faith in interventions that those we seek to help may be among the biggest impediments to progress. We cannot simply fail to intervene in messy situations when we have interests that we need to protect. We will have to be even more aggressively conditional in the disbursement of our economic, diplomatic, and military capital, making our terms crystal clear going in, being willing to withdraw our commitment at the first sign of a wrong move, and either being committed enough unilaterally to have true leverage, or being confident that we can manage our fellow international community members in such a way that they will support our efforts.

We must also explore means by which to distribute more of our aid directly to the private sector in recipient countries—circumventing the local governments—and to make the fair, independent administration of our programs a prerequisite to the provision of aid. This will frustrate local politicians seeking to gain the benefit of distributing rewards to their constituents, but if such local counterparts fail to support us and we cannot count on our allies in the international community, then direct administration of private sector programs (by agencies that understand the business community rather than the NGO community) would be of great value. The "problem of the uncooperative beneficiary" is likely to be faced repeatedly, and it alone can undermine peacekeeping efforts even when all else goes according to plan.

Other strategic analyses must consider the following questions: Do our economic programs support nationalism or pluralism? Are the opponents of our plans undermined by our efforts? If there are several possible outcomes of a situation, how do our actions affect each? What will our economic efforts mean when the troops are gone? At the same time, we must be careful to calculate how ethnic conflicts are different from other kinds of conflicts—and careful not to overestimate the impact of economic initiatives in such situations. When ethnic divisions have withstood the major historical transformations that have taken place over the centuries, it is unlikely that even substantial economic upticks will make for profound change. Instead, we must see them for what they are—palliatives required if momentary crises are not to grow worse.

CONCLUSION 3: MAKE
A VISIBLE DIFFERENCE

Rapid deployment of resources to visible projects is key: it builds political will.

Realistic and timely economic planning drawing on the full resources of the U.S. government requires a keen recognition of priorities. Indeed, inattention to communicating successes and building political will have dogged many of our international recovery efforts.

Most current tools for economic intervention are traditional aid organizations that concentrate on long-term development. In emergency interventions, however, it is more important to set short-term, publicizable objectives and meet them in order to cement the local population's commitment to the new order (and the commitment of the taxpayers of the intervening countries to continued aid).

A recovery can be actively undermined if its positive outcomes are kept under a bushel basket. Better, more effective communications programs aimed at stimulating political support in the U.S., as well as among our friends and allies on the ground (including new governments such as the one in Haiti) are urgently needed. We must also avoid inflated expectations by being realistic from the start in order to keep popular support for our efforts high.

While resources for both rapid and longer-term deployment are essential, resources alone will not suffice. Will and realism on the supply side must also be added to the mix. Given the budget- and deficit-cutting environment of the U.S. Congress, money is exceptionally tight. The political situation is not much more promising: Opponents of the President have in the past and will again attempt to restrict resources to influence or kill programs for which there is not broad support. In addition, the Haiti experience shows that—due to flagging political attention spans in the U.S. and the desire to get risks off the table as quickly as possible—long-term commitments are nearly impossible to obtain.

The battle for greater discretionary aid funding must be re-engaged. Many seem to have decided that pressing for increased aid funding is politically unviable. The fact remains that no major nation spends a smaller portion of GDP on aid than does the United States—and yet, as the world's leader, we have greater and increasing responsibilities in this regard. Mobilizing international money is not an effective substitute for disbursing funds that the United States can program and manage, and control of these funds ultimately has proven to be one of the more effective levers at Washington's disposal for influencing the decisions of our "partners." Maximizing economic leverage over such partners is a critical control mechanism if future efforts are to be fully effective.

Furthermore, in cases of national importance—particularly in cases where economic recovery can shorten the mission of U.S. soldiers, otherwise reduce risks for those soldiers, or reduce the likelihood of the return of such soldiers to a dangerous environment—a special discretionary fund should be established. The discretionary fund would allow the president to finance new and often fluid needs without the demand for re-programming or the need to return to Congress when time is of the essence.

We must re-evaluate our aid spending priorities: to wit, more focus, more private sector. Recognizing that funding will be tight regardless of any success in advancing proposals such as those raised above, it is important to better live within our limitations. The United States has the most far-flung and diffuse aid program of any major aid donor. Fewer recipients should be designated for our aid support, more money should be held in reserve for emergency situations, and the design of programs that have measurable foreign policy results should be at the forefront of the minds of planners.

Prudence and realism also suggest that more emphasis should be placed on supporting private sector needs, thus priming the pump for future foreign and domestic investment and thereby stimulating sustainable, non–aid driven growth. AID used to have programs that accomplished as much, but they finally died in the early 1990s after years of inter-agency warfare. The function should be restored, although it would be better located in Commerce, the center of private sector policy planning in the government, than in AID or State.

SHOW ME THE MONEY

In Haiti, the challenges to political will-building came because few Haitians read newspapers or watch television, and Creole radio broadcasts, town meetings, church, and other of the more effective grassroots communications tools were underutilized. Such a failure to communicate renders progress invisible to wider populations. Furthermore, effective communication leverages the impact of even modest achievements at a comparatively low cost.

The principal concerns of the donor group in Haiti were, as noted earlier, those "visible differences" that were identified as being most crucial. The most important included restoration of the power sector (thus providing dependable power to Port-au-Prince and to manufacturing installations), the letting of cellular telecommunications contracts (which afforded the fastest possible way to improve the weak telecommunications infrastructure), and the initiation of privatization efforts among the nine key parastatals—notably the ports, the telephone company, Electricité d'Haiti, the flour mill, and the cement factory. Job creation through the rebirth of the assembly sector would come if these steps were achieved, stability maintained, and red tape eliminated.

Efforts in each of these areas were tortured and ranged from minimal success (Haiti, which requires about 100 megawatts of power, now can depend on 60-plus in the dry season, up from a low of 20 or so) to utter stagnation (everything else). Promises were made, but in key areas the U.S. government ran into the biggest obstacle to its efforts to help Haiti: the very government that it had helped to reinstall. In the words of former U.S. Ambassador to Haiti Ernest Preeg in his February 28, 1996, testimony to Congress, "the Aristide government's record was one of brave words but almost total non-performance on economic reforms." He went on to say:

> The economic outlook for the Préval government is thus exceedingly grave. Unemployment in Port-au-Prince is 70-80 percent—creating a political tinderbox—while the extraordinarily high aid disbursements of 1995 are in rapid decline. U.S. aid to Haiti will drop from $235 million in fiscal year 1995 to $80-90 million in 1996 (which alone equates with a drop of 7-10 percent in Haitian GDP), and other aid donors are insisting on concrete implementation of economic reforms before continuing their disbursements. Meanwhile, the large majority of impoverished Haitian people are legitimately asking what happened to all of the much-heralded aid flowing into the country. The unfortunate answer is that most of it, because of non-performance by the Aristide government, has been squandered on temporary relief with no lasting effect, particularly through budget support to the public sector payroll.

The need for assistance programs to make a highly visible difference and to set practical objectives is a self-explanatory lesson of the age of limitations. It is possible to list everything that must be done or everything that should be done. But it is impossible to actually do either— especially in the very limited window of opportunity presented in post-intervention situations. A few key objectives must be set and pursued. It should be noted here that one of the most significant failures of our efforts in Haiti was not communicating effectively just how limited the window of opportunity was. In many respects, it has already shut. Foreign aid inflows such as those in 1995 (over $600 million, a third to a half of Haiti's GDP) will never be seen again. Indeed, foreign aid from sources other than the United States fell over $160 million from 1995 to 1996 alone. Moreover, should crisis recur, the ability to muster U.S. support for a government and people that have squandered a prior opportunity is greatly diminished.

THE UNSUITABILITY OF TRADITIONAL DEVELOPMENT MODELS FOR EMERGENCY ASSISTANCE

Multilateral development banks and aid organizations viewed the problems they faced in post-crisis situations in traditional development terms, focusing on long-term social and infrastructure issues and taking great care to have "quality projects" and to ensure minimum waste (by their standards). They did not stop to consider that their delays could take such a toll on the political situation on the ground and that their careful calculations and "quality controls" would be rendered meaningless by systemic reversals. In both Haiti and the Middle East, it was not realized until after a lengthy period of frustration and growing political discontent that more focus was required on the kinds of high-impact projects that could happen quickly and send a strong message to the local populace that the new situation was in their interest.

In the Middle East, problems such as those just described with respect to Haiti contributed to the sense of crisis that gripped the international aid program after just over a year. By late 1994 and early 1995, the United States joined the other donor nations in calling for a refocus and restructuring of donor efforts. A Local Aid Coordination Committee (LACC) was created that played aid traffic cop on the ground in the Territories, as was a Joint Liaison Committee to resolve problems between the donors and the principals on the ground. As McGill University Professor Rex Brynen reports:

> Donors recognized the political importance of "quick disbursing job creation projects" and at the local level the various LACC sectoral working groups focused greater attention on the actual number of "person working days" generated by each project . . . Some donors also looked to new mechanisms for communicating to Palestinians the benefits of the peace process. One of the most successful examples of this has been a series of new public areas in Gaza. With their highly visible green spaces and playground equipment, these have been hugely successful psychological indicators of positive change associated with peace. (*Journal of Palestine Studies*, Spring 1996.)

Brynen adds that the World Bank significantly revamped its structure to speed the delivery of the assistance. In addition, the United Nations gave tremendous spending flexibility to a Special Coordinator on the ground who had to answer to no one in the U.N. apparatus but the Secretary-General. At the same time, the U.N. Relief and Works Agency (UNRWA) adopted policies allowing it essentially to launder money, which could then be used to pay for police salaries. Donor countries also became more creative. For example, the German government found ways to circumvent legislation preventing budget support for the Palestinians by donating office supplies and toilet paper to Arafat rather than Deutsche marks.

New priorities must be set that recognize the real-world demands of emergency assistance programs. This is not to say that long-term development should always take a back seat to near-term issues. However, near-term imperatives for tangible results must take priority sufficiently frequently to assure the political will to move forward with peace and stability. Maximum impact programs should be given priority. Their exact nature will change from situation to situation. In many cases, these projects will involve job creation. In some, they will involve rebuilding key elements of infrastructure, restoring power or water, rebuilding a bridge, or building a park. Even as these steps are taken, an equally intensive and professional effort must take place to communicate their results to the intended populations—those whose will the programs must harness. It is important to consider economic activity that is already present on the ground and encourage it (i.e., through expanded micro-lending programs). Furthermore, it is essential to recognize opportunities that are created by enhanced market access and to develop them as aggressively as the situation dictates. Also, it is important to remember that taking unusual risks is just part of the post-intervention recovery process.

We should not be obsessed with meeting bureaucratic criteria for project quality at the expense of losing political momentum critical to the overall success of the intervention. Many multilateral-organization mechanisms are designed to assure transparency, to maximize "efficient" utilization of funds, and to ensure that projects meet certain standards. While these criteria should not be overlooked in a cavalier way, neither should they be blindly followed. Visible results that are politically meaningful within a target population cannot be sacrificed or indefinitely postponed to satisfy well-intentioned bureaucratic criteria. Part of being realistic is showing tolerance (to a certain degree) for the limitations and methods of recipients like Arafat.

POST-DAYTON ECONOMIC EFFORTS:
A DROP IN A SEA OF TROUBLES

In Bosnia, the facts that the cease-fire has largely been honored and that several rounds of elections have been held are signs that progress is being made—even if the elections were imperfect and the results contested. At the same time, however, in terms of the everyday needs of the Bosnian people—the "ideology of the light bulb"—efforts thus far have produced negligible results. In many if not most villages and towns, clean, safe water and sewage systems are memories or promises. Perhaps two-thirds of all the country's water supply is lost through damage to viaducts, pumping stations, pipelines, and other facilities. Electric power production is at just 20 percent of its 1990 level, coal production half that. Virtually all electric distribution capacity has been destroyed. One phone call in a hundred goes through; 100,000 lines have been lost; and only a tenth of the pre-war quota of 4,000 international lines remains active. According to journalist Amy Kaslow:

> ". . . foreign glass suppliers are shipping enough glass to Bosnia to create a meter high wall from London to Paris," says Mark Cotts, UNHCR's Sarajevo chief, who is managing the project. "We're putting in a total of 400,000 square meters of glass over a six month period," Cotts says. But UNHCR's work will satisfy just 30 percent of the capital city's needs, without addressing those of the rest of the country. (*Infrastructure Finance*, Vol. 5, No. 6, September 9, 1996, p. 18.)

The World Bank estimates the total damage sustained by Bosnia to have an economic cost in excess of $25 billion. The Bosnian government puts the toll at twice that. The international donor community has developed a reconstruction plan that targets $5.1 billion in assistance during the first five years after the Dayton agreement—big money by international reconstruction standards, but, in the words of one Bosnian official, "a drop in the ocean" compared to what is needed.

Furthermore, of that $5.1 billion, less than $2 billion was actually committed by the end of 1996. And of that $2 billion, only about 75 percent has been targeted for specific projects. Of more than $1 billion in projects planned for 1996, only about $600-700 million had actually been disbursed by the end of 1996, with contracts for a further $144 million signed. One hundred million dollars from the Japanese was "missing in inaction." Four hundred million dollars from Islamic countries is untraceable—not having traveled directly to governments or through channels that the other donors can identify. The U.S. Congress has dragged its feet with appropriations, and the Europeans have done little better. Thus, as of the end of 1996, the amount of international donor money that had actually made its way down from the international podiums onto the streets of Bosnia was estimated at between $250 million and $400 million, with the latter number almost certainly being too high. (As of the end of 1997, $2.6 billion was committed, about 80 percent of which has been targeted for specific projects.)

At the two donor conferences, commitment patterns were interesting and would later be a source of tension. Russia pledged more than France, Germany, or the United Kingdom—more, in fact, than France and Germany combined. Norway, too, contributed more than those European Union (EU) leaders, and Switzerland almost as much. The United States committed over a quarter of a billion dollars, more by far than any other single nation. In fact, non-EU donors gave more than twice as much as the EU countries' $347 million. This was compensated for by a major commitment by the EU itself, but even considering that, the flows from outside Europe almost equaled those from within. The most striking thing about these figures is the fact that while they may represent the fair share from the United States, they do not give us great leverage within the donor mix.

Pledges and disbursements are vastly different things. Expectations raised by the pledges were later frustrated when dollars flowed in much more slowly than anyone anticipated. A June 1996 report from the World Bank and the European Union commented on this fact, just as the international community's civilian High Representative Carl Bildt had done for months. The report said that "several key donors have not yet committed all or part of their funds. This goes against the consensus of the Brussels Donors Conference framework; namely, that *timing is everything* [emphasis in original]; assistance must be front-loaded to ensure a visible 'peace dividend' before the elections."

U.S. assistance to Bosnia during the first full year of post-Dayton implementation came in the form of several types of pledges. The sum of $148 million was to be directed to economic reconstruction and revitalization, $12.5 million to emergency shelter repair, $8.5 million to demining, and $50 million to police training and monitors. These amounts were offered at the April 1996 Brussels Donors Conference, in addition to the $62.7 million that had been pledged previously. Thus, the total U.S. commitment to the priority reconstruction program was $281.7 million. Beyond the U.S. funds going for reconstruction, we committed $149.3 million to on-going humanitarian and relief programs, and the U.S. contribution to international support for the elections, police monitors, peacekeeping, and the war crimes tribunal totaled $119 million. The total pledged by the United States for 1996 was $550 million. Of this, 65-80 percent has been obligated, and only a fraction of that has actually been disbursed. Furthermore, it is interesting that less than half of this amount was to be directed to the kind of fast-disbursing reconstruction projects that allegedly were, and should have been, the central objective of the overall effort if the peace dividend was to be achieved.

WHEN EXPECTATIONS EXCEED ACTIONS

It is vital that U.S. policy-makers recognize the danger of unrealistic expectations. The formation of donor groups and the initiation of donor activities inevitably result from situations of great drama—either a crisis or a breakthrough—and such situations generate euphoria that distorts perspectives and expectations. This can leave a devastatingly heavy burden on future initiatives. In each of the major cases discussed here, promises were made of over $1 billion in aid in the first year of the effort, and in each case the money flowed like molasses. Political opponents on the ground used broken promises to their advantage.

Putting our focus on at least three key areas could have fostered the success of the U.S. interventions in Haiti, the Middle East, and Bosnia, and it can improve the effectiveness of future interventions. First, we must do more to integrate economic and military initiatives. Separation of the economic and military components of our efforts in Bosnia undoubtedly was linked to our desire to have unadulterated control of the military apparatus and our understanding that having such control would be impossible on the economic side. Yet armies build bridges, ensure the free flow of workers, restore power plants and telephone systems, and can provide the fast results that are demanded to achieve the short-term political needs in emergency situations.

Second, in cases like Bosnia, where integration into the surrounding economic environment is key, the prospective formation of regional trading blocs and associations and of links with existing organizations should be cultivated, and the levers associated with possible memberships should be used more strategically to support objectives such as those targeted through conditionality of the type refered to throughout this book. Bosnia's association with the Central European Free Trade Association (CEFTA) and/or the EU and a clear path to such associations, for example, could offer real hope to businesses and investors. It is foolish to think that such agreements could be immediately meaningful at every possible level to an economy as devastated as Bosnia's, but it would give donors a meaningful "carrot" and could offer other benefits in terms of helping get a handle on problems in Kosovo, Macedonia, and beyond.

Third, it is very important that we develop a program to counteract the brain drain suffered by Bosnia and other countries experiencing external conflict. Security and the promise of economic development are prerequisites. But concrete offers of housing or work or tax incentives to return should be considered, because if the best and the brightest remain abroad, Bosnia's recovery will be seriously and indefinitely impeded.

A process driven by intense public outrage and/or interest, typically a short-term phenomenon, is no match for one undergirded by an integrated planning process, incorporating lessons learned along with a realistic assessment of specific needs and obstacles. The money must be there; but so must there be an understanding of how timing effects on-the-ground reality.

The special economic measures required in emergency interventions take on the political rather than economic characteristics. In this case, all economics becomes local. Projects must be undertaken with specific communities in mind and specific responses sought. Like contemporary politics, emergency economics is tied to the moment—it must solve today's problem now. Instant gratification is the goal. Emergency economics must also fit into a sound bite. If the value of the project has to be explained, if it can't be easily communicated in a way that cuts straight to the gut, it probably won't have the desired impact. Like politics, emergency economics loves a winner. A string of success stories puts momentum on the side of the peacekeepers. The public asks the same thing of emergency economic initiatives that it asks of politicians: "What have you done for me lately?"

CONCLUSION 4: IMPROVE U.S. EFFECTIVENESS IN MULTILATERAL CONTEXTS

We must learn to work more effectively in a multilateral context—as must the other members of the donor community.

We must recognize that, given limitations on U.S. budgets, many key foreign policy initiatives will require that we influence and often lead multilateral efforts in conjunction with our own national efforts. Involvement in multilateral efforts will stretch our resources and test not only our diplomatic skills but also our ability to set clear priorities and assess risks and goals. We must especially rise above or otherwise manage petty rivalries with other donors so that our focus stays on successfully completing the work at hand. Better multilateral structures also need to be built to carry common goals when international actors do reach agreement.

A multilateral process was necessary to raise the funding amounts needed to support rebuilding in all three cases. Unlike the aftermath of the Camp David process, in which the United States simply wrote the checks to Israel and Egypt and thus had far greater control over outcomes on the economic side, in Haiti and the Middle East in the 1990s, the U.S. government was hard-pressed by internal budgetary constraints to provide more than a lead donor's contribution to the funding effort. This left both initiatives in large part in the hands of donor committees, multilateral development banks, NGOs, independent funds, and other complex and unwieldy entities. In both cases, disbursal of funds was slower than expected, coordination was extremely difficult, and the United States had a hard time tailoring initiatives to its specific objectives. In addition, there were "rival" peacemakers in both cases who had somewhat different agendas from Washington, making matters even more complex. Moreover, in both Haiti and the Middle East, relations between multilateral groups and the local authorities often were strained when the promises of donors inflated expectations but failed to translate into reality.

A MULTILATERAL MORASS IN THE MIDDLE EAST

Just two weeks after the signings on the White House lawn, an international donors meeting was convened in Paris to develop and coordinate a plan for the distribution of aid to the Palestinian Territories and for the stimulation of economic growth to support the peace process. Such meetings, held hard on the heels of major agreements, are always in jeopardy of being driven at least as much by hope as by experience. However, in this particular case, given the dramatic nature of the agreements that had just been signed—such a breakthrough would have been inconceivable only a few years earlier—the donors conference initiated a process in which euphoria would produce not only large promises of aid—initially $2.1 billion, later growing to $2.6 billion—but miscalculations about the economic and overall prospects of the Territories, about the likely speed of their recovery, and about their specific cash and capital needs.

As was the case in Haiti and as has been true in other similar situations, the donor process began with unjustified assumptions that the aid money being channeled into the Palestinian Territories would be used to lay the foundations of long-term prosperity. Infrastructure would be built. The private sector would follow with major investments. Economic recovery and the establishment of needed institutions would come relatively quickly. The new entity would, in a matter of a year or two, begin to operate like the established bureaucracy it was replacing.

As noted by Barbara Balaj, Ishac Diwan, and Bernard Philippe in their 1995 article, "External Assistance to the Palestinians: What Went Wrong?" in *Politique Etrangère*:

> In the original plan, investments in infrastructure were supposed to consume the lion's share of donor pledges, with smaller expenditures on recurrent items to help establish the new Palestinian Authority, and some technical assistance to put together the institutions and blueprints necessary for an infrastructure boom. But, two years later, investments consumed only about one-half of the originally projected amounts. On the other hand, the amounts allocated to the financing of recurrent expenditures were 2.5 times more than initially anticipated.

As a result, of the $370 million programmed for public investment from 1994 through mid-1995, only about $205 million actually went for that purpose, whereas $240 million, rather than just over $100 million, went for budget assistance. Furthermore, the original plan expected budget deficits to disappear by 1995. This has not happened, and deficits were seen in 1996 and 1997.

The slowness of the distribution process can be attributed in large part to the international resonance of this mission. For example, in the first two years of the effort, twenty-seven donors were responsible for committing the just over $400 million in recurrent costs. The overall program drew in almost 40 different international organizations and countries which, in turn, had to work with hundreds of non-governmental organizations and the various local authorities. If individual governments acting alone suffer from bureaucratic snags, tangles, misjudgments, and turf wars, imagine trying to orchestrate so many other actors.

Unfortunately, no imagination is required. The history of the multilateral aid process in the Middle East stands as a monument to the tangled web that even the best-intentioned governments weave (see Figure 1). While the international community clearly had deep pockets in this case and could respond in times of crisis—which was good, given the initial misassumptions and the volatility of the situation on the ground—each country had to deal with its own political issues, reluctant parliaments, aid priorities, standards, credit needs, and desire to be seen as driving the process. (The United States suffered particularly in this regard in the form of congressional demands to periodically review compliance with the Oslo agreements and regular haggling over all aid programs as a consequence of efforts to restructure our entire aid apparatus.) The accompanying figure—from McGill University Professor Rex Brynen's excellent article on this subject, "The (Very) Political Economy of the West Bank and Gaza: Learning Lessons About Peace-Building and Development Assistance" (Montreal Studies on the Contemporary Arab World, March 1996)—illustrates the situation in the starkest possible way. Covering the international side of this question extremely well, Brynen also notes several problems with the assumptions that guided the international donor community: "Initial donor assumptions were often 'very facile' [in the words of one World Bank official], underestimating the political and economic difficulties that lay ahead. Israeli closure of the territories and the institutional growing pains of the PA, for example, were largely unanticipated."

The convoluted nature of the donor process and the search for a better way also led to a familiar nostalgia among some critics for initiatives like the Marshall Plan or even the Camp David support efforts, in which one nation took the clear lead. This is a common phenomenon. It is also one with serious implications for the United States, which is really the only nation in a position to take such a lead in many international matters. Our unwillingness to do so effectively precludes such leadership from taking place. This in turn places the future of such efforts in the hands of complicated multilateral authorities such as the one that undertook the economic reconstruction program in the Palestinian Territories.

U.S. policy-makers have three options: take the lead when it is essential that an intervention be done precisely to U.S. specifications; learn to lead within multilateral fora when compromise and broad-based support are possible; or, in circumstances when crucial U.S.

WEST BANK AND GAZA:
ORGANIZATIONAL SCHEMA OF ASSISTANCE PROGRAM

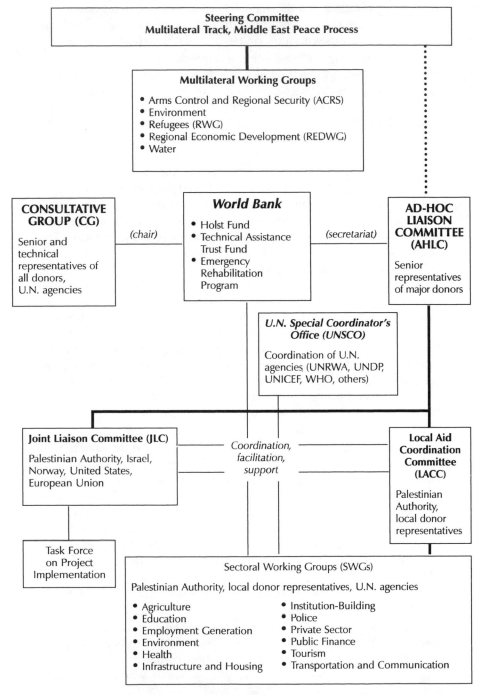

Steering Committee
Multilateral Track, Middle East Peace Process

Multilateral Working Groups

- Arms Control and Regional Security (ACRS)
- Environment
- Refugees (RWG)
- Regional Economic Development (REDWG)
- Water

CONSULTATIVE GROUP (CG)

Senior and technical representatives of all donors, U.N. agencies

(chair)

World Bank

- Holst Fund
- Technical Assistance Trust Fund
- Emergency Rehabilitation Program

(secretariat)

AD-HOC LIAISON COMMITTEE (AHLC)

Senior representatives of major donors

U.N. Special Coordinator's Office (UNSCO)

Coordination of U.N. agencies (UNRWA, UNDP, UNICEF, WHO, others)

Joint Liaison Committee (JLC)

Palestinian Authority, Israel, Norway, United States, European Union

Coordination, facilitation, support

Local Aid Coordination Committee (LACC)

Palestinian Authority, local donor representatives

Task Force on Project Implementation

Sectoral Working Groups (SWGs)

Palestinian Authority, local donor representatives, U.N. agencies

- Agriculture
- Education
- Employment Generation
- Environment
- Health
- Infrastructure and Housing
- Institution-Building
- Police
- Private Sector
- Public Finance
- Tourism
- Transportation and Communication

Source: Rex Brynen (McGill University). "The (Very) Political Economy of the West Bank and Gaza," *Montreal Studies on the Contemporary Arab World* (Montreal: Inter-University Consortium for Arab Studies, March 1996). Chart also on Palestinian InfoNet (www.arts.mcgill.ca/mepp/mepp.html).

national interests are not at stake but it is important to show the flag, contribute and set our expectations at appropriately low levels. Given the U.S. government's important if not defining role in the multilateral donor process in the Middle East (we were the number one donor among individual nations, with a pledge of $500 million, just behind the EU's $600 million and well ahead of all other individual nations) and the organizational and policy problems that these donors faced or inflicted upon the situation, the idea that more effective political leadership on the part of Washington will necessarily produce a better outcome must be suspect. Sound analysis and effective emergency economic policy formation are also needed.

Despite the best efforts of many dedicated officials, the economic component of the post-Oslo effort has been only sporadically successful. The problems began with the multilateral donor process. Here, the United States, represented by AID, not only bought into the badly misjudged assumptions of the donor plan but also failed to press conditionality in a meaningful way, failed to bring order to the chaotic process of coordinating donor efforts, and failed, at least at the outset, to identify the proper priorities for the effort.

In addition, the United States was as guilty as other nations of jockeying for influence within the donor process and creating unproductive rivalries, most notably with the EU. The EU, as the "leading" donor in dollar terms, felt that it deserved a corresponding role in the peace process. The United States, given its traditional mediating role, the size of its other regional aid programs, and its strategic importance, felt differently. This rivalry also manifested itself in an entirely unhelpful way on the diplomatic side of the peace process and, not surprisingly, in active competition for certain major commercial projects.

Given the likelihood that more and more U.S. international initiatives will require similar coalitions and depend in a similar way on "other people's money," managing relationships with other competing donors so that they don't become destructive is going to become especially important.

A further source of tension in donor relationships has been the differing approaches to winning some of the reconstruction contracts. In the Bosnia case, for example, U.S. and British companies alike have complained that some countries were offering tied-aid packages, which guaranteed that deals would be awarded to their domestic firms. According to the *Financial Times:*

> Mr. John Davie, a project manager with Vector, the aviation and transport management consultants, said, "Sweden and the Netherlands have tied bilateral aid to ensure their domestic com-

panies win telecommunications contracts and work on rebuilding Sarajevo airport. The Germans have also been very active in this area." (July 16, 1996, p. 8.)

When the United States determines that it is in its interest not only to promote economic development but to win an increasing share of that development for our companies (thus providing essential political support for such efforts back home), it has to become more aggressive as well.

U.S. policy-makers must also re-evaluate multilateral donor structures in the same way that we contemplate re-evaluating our own emergency aid mechanisms. Both the international effort to aid the peace process in the Palestinian Territories and the concurrent U.S. efforts to that same end did something unusual and important during the past four years: They changed course. The designers of both recognized that there were substantial problems in their execution and planning, and they made mid-course corrections that have been helpful, even if they in turn were overtaken by other events that marginalized many economic programs.

Big donor groups should be effectively driven by a single steering committee of wieldy size. A liaison group should be established on the ground that can expedite problem-solving, break bottlenecks, mediate disputes, and cope with institutional problems that are presented by recipient governments. One possible solution would be to create individually incorporated enterprise funds.

Even in the best of circumstances (i.e., a unanimity of donor intentions), the organizations utilized in past and present efforts have often fallen far short of what is necessary. For example, looking to a previous intervention in Mozambique, the United Nations bureaucracy, which is not noted for its flexibility and speed of action, has presented a significant obstacle. In addition, the United Nations created new bureaucracies to deal with the activities in Mozambique instead of using existing agencies such as the U.N. Development Programme (UNDP), the U.N. High Commissioner for Refugees (UNHCR), and the World Food Programme. Still more problems arose from the lack of clear lines of authority and insufficient operational responsibility vested in the organizations on the ground. As a result, much time and money was wasted in consultations with and approvals from the head offices in New York.

MULTIPLE VISIONS, MULTIPLE
FRUSTRATIONS IN BOSNIA

The U.N. mandate in Bosnia was limited, and its forces were hamstrung by disagreements among the major powers involved. Humanitarian aid poured in—perhaps $8 billion since the onset of the conflict following the collapse of the former Yugoslavia, though only a fraction of what was needed—and slowly the international community, led by the United States, was forced to step in more decisively. The eventual result was the Dayton Accords, which brought an end to the war, set borders, and envisioned the civil transformation of Bosnia—the development of democracy, including elections; the establishment of a constitutional structure and effective police forces; and the capture and prosecution of war criminals.

The Dayton Accords came about largely because, unlike past efforts, the negotiations not only brought to bear the full force of the U.S. government but also brought to the table the leaders of Serbia and Croatia, who had played such crucial roles in waging the war that devastated Bosnia. Dayton's primary architect, Richard Holbrooke, and others acknowledge that, in this mix of former combatants and reluctant allies at Dayton, one of the key factors motivating Serbian leader Slobodan Milosevic to agree to the Accords was the lifting of crushing multilateral economic sanctions against his nation. Largely with this and territorial considerations in mind, he signed the peace agreement in Paris in mid-December 1995.

In that same month and again four months later, in April, donors from around the world met to pledge an initial tranche of over $1.8 billion for the recovery of Bosnia. That money was to be used in the first year of the five-year program devised to address the most serious infrastructure challenges facing Bosnia. The $5.1 billion program included $380 million for water and sanitation, $893 million for energy, $698 million for transport, $567 million for telecommunications, $330 million for agriculture, $400 million for industry, $275 million for education, $540 million for health, $600 million for housing, $200 million for demining, and $210 million for social support.

It was agreed that the focus of all efforts should quickly shift from humanitarian to reconstruction assistance, that all sectors must be improved to avoid bottlenecks, that jobs are a top priority—particularly those for demobilized soldiers—and that domestic suppliers, contractors, and companies are to be used wherever possible to maximize the benefit of the aid flows. There was also to be an emphasis on trade in addition to aid. A debate began almost immediately as to whether a free trade area should be established within the Balkans, how these countries might affiliate to the CEFTA group of countries, and when they might aspire to associate status within the EU. Emphasis also was placed on building key public sector institutions, privatizing banks and enterprises, and raising domestic savings and public revenues.

Even with these goals apparently decided upon, tensions soon arose among the donors. The tensions took several forms. At the most superficial level, they were manifested in simple competition among the donors for primacy in the fund administration and strategic decision-making process—a role that had been given to the EU at Dayton. Had merely turf conflicts developed, they would have been little more than nuisances, but starting within weeks of Dayton, fundamental strategic differences emerged between the Europeans and the Americans. What happened has been chronicled widely. In the July 1996 issue of *Transition*, Susan Woodward of the Brookings Institution described the problem this way:

> Regarding the economic assistance that is considered essential to consolidate the peace, the United States has insisted on giving to the Croat-Muslim Federation alone and on isolating the Bosnian Serbs. The Europeans counter that economic reconstruction must occur throughout the country and must aim to reintegrate its parts, if the goal is peace and a single country.
>
> The Pentagon insisted on a complete separation between military and civilian aspects rather than the integration that Europeans with peacekeeping experience knew was necessary, and it blamed Europeans for delays in the civilian operation. The Europeans insisted that the cause of such delays was that very separation and tardy American commitment of funds for civilian (as opposed to military) tasks and assistance.

Woodward cited battles in back rooms at Dayton over these issues and continuing battles throughout the months since, concluding that:

> The fighting has been replaced by differing perspectives on the use of conditionality—withholding funds until parties have complied with particular obligations as opposed to using economic assistance as a positive incentive to entice cooperation, withdrawing it later if the parties do not comply—and whether instituting harsher conditions for the Republika Srpska is a counterproductive tactic in the long run.
>
> American calls at the 2 June (1996) summit in Geneva to reimpose sanctions on Serbia proper if President Slobodan Milosevic does not hand over the two [indicted war criminals Karadzic and Mladic] will compound the dispute. Europeans have already

established diplomatic relations with the Federal Republic of Yugoslavia [the United States has not]. And they now see sanctions as essentially unenforceable and counterproductive.

In the words of one European diplomat, "The war is over, the peace has been signed, but the Americans insist on their policy of punishing and humiliating the Serbs."

Does such behavior on the part of the United States advance the peace and our national interests? This is debatable, although it is my strong feeling that it does and that we should not compound past errors of appeasement from previous administrations and from our allies in Europe with continuing weakness today. What is clear is that the division between the United States and Europe on this front threatens the peace process; undermines our credibility with local governments that must be forced into compliance with the political, economic, and judicial terms of Dayton; and therefore is, at some level, indicative of a failure to implement our foreign policy.

The United States cannot hope to achieve peace through international coalitions if we cannot manage those coalitions. Either we do this through the application of all of our military, diplomatic, and economic leverage or through consenting to our partners' positions from time to time. The way it has been done in Bosnia is indicative of yet another current political reality complicating our peacekeeping efforts: our inability to reconcile our view of ourselves as world leader with the limitations imposed upon us by our budget and domestic political imperatives.

While the Europeans and Americans have fought among themselves, other actors with more dubious intentions have not been inactive—as stories during 1996 about covert arms agreements between the Bosnian Muslims and Turkey, Malaysia, and Iran demonstrate.

There were more basic disagreements among the allies than those over their approaches to aid. One concerned the issue of self-determination. This is an important issue; as we consider the economic reconstruction of Bosnia, we must ask what it is that we are trying to reconstruct. Is Bosnia to be a multi-ethnic state? Bosnia has never existed independently of a larger national entity with ways and means to enforce stability. Is it to consist of ethnic mini-states within a federative framework? If so, then building the infrastructure links between those mini-states and their patron states is perhaps more important than building links among the effectively separate entities. If our goal was to preserve the weakest of those entities to provide a balance against the strongest, then perhaps we should have focused our efforts on the Bosniak rump state that could have emerged.

A careful effort must be made to understand how the promotion of infrastructure redevelopment (or development) can stimulate the integration or disintegration of a formative political entity or society. In Bosnia, the differences among donors regarding their missions, their ultimate goals (a multi-ethnic state? ethnic mini-states? strong associations with Serbia and Croatia? or weak ones?), and other issues suggest that the maximum effect of the economic intervention will not be achieved. Indeed, different agencies and governments have been working at cross-purposes.

LEADERSHIP IN AN AGE OF LIMITED RESOURCES

Even if a consensus answer to these questions did exist within the U.S. government—and it does not—there is real doubt as to whether the questions are ours to answer. All agree, however, that the current peace would not be possible without the leadership and military commitment of the United States. Consequently, we have been able to set the terms for the military side of this operation with considerable success.

On the economic side of the equation, the kinds of tensions that arose among donors in Haiti and the Middle East were exacerbated in Bosnia by the strong American sense that this was a European problem and that Europeans should foot the bill. Since Washington did not want to accept a leadership role in funding the civilian component of the operation, we had to bring together a coalition to do so. Again, as in Haiti, we were compelled to use "other people's money," thereby necessarily ceding some control. And again, as in Haiti and the Middle East, we were compelled to give that money to the local governments, which might or might not use it in ways that we deem constructive.

In the Middle East, the United States was immediately thrust into a leadership role in the peace-building effort. The importance of assuming this role was little debated in the United States. It was understood that without active U.S. intervention, the promise of peace symbolized by the ceremony on the White House lawn could not be made real.

Here we see one of the most important distinctions between the Middle East peace situation and the other "peacekeeping" or post-crisis interventions that are the subject of this study. In the cases of both Haiti and Bosnia, there was great uncertainty in the United States about the appropriate role for the U.S. government. Public support in the United States for intervention in Haiti and Bosnia was spotty at best, and in each case American policy-makers were uncertain what course of action made the most sense. Should troops be sent in? With what mission? For what duration? In what relationship to troops from allied nations?

Should the United States intervene in other ways to assist the peace process? With what commitment of resources? In coordination with what international agencies? Indeed, in both Haiti and Bosnia, the fundamental question underlying all foreign policy decisions—where do our national interests lie?—was difficult to answer to the satisfaction of a large portion of the American people.

America must lead or accept other leadership. Before the intervention begins, U.S. policy-makers must decide how much the effort means to us and then act accordingly. If they decide that there are certain goals that must be accomplished, then the United States must be prepared to dedicate its international muscle and its force of will toward marshaling other nations. If we are not willing or able to take the necessary steps to lead effectively, we should be willing to step back and learn to accept a new and different role in multilateral efforts—one in which our goals are the development of consensus and the search for others to take the lead, and in which we seek to practice diplomatic democracy rather than last-remaining-superpower autocracy.

And if the U.S. Congress assures us such a backseat role by limiting resources, then legislators, too, must adjust their expectations of our leverage and impact in post-crisis situations. Not doing so will only continue to make the situation on the ground as confusing and frustrating as it has been in Haiti, the Middle East, and Bosnia.

CONCLUSION 5:
GET THE RIGHT TOOLS

Businesses follow the market, not foreign policy initiatives. New financial tools designed to fund private sector projects in high-risk venues are needed.

Only effective bottom-line incentives will draw businesses into post-crisis or transitional (high-risk) situations. The U.S. government should not—as it has in the recent past—expect them to do the heavy lifting or to fill the void created by a lack of official resources or will.

U.S. policy-makers must not fall victim to the mythologies of private sector investment. Such investment is crucial to sustainable growth. But without government programs that will create real incentives for companies to undertake considerable risk in transitional or unstable situations, the private sector will not undertake investments simply because it is in the best interests of a country or a region for them to do so. The U.S. government should swim against the current tide of anti-corporate welfare and anti–foreign aid sentiment to encourage not only the maintenance of OPIC risk insurance programs but the establishment of new, special-situation, high-risk investment insurance programs to aid recovery in post-crisis environments.

The programs of the Overseas Private Investment Corporation (OPIC), the Export-Import Bank (ExIm), the Trade and Development Agency (TDA), or any other existing U.S. agency are not specifically designed to attract U.S. companies and investors to high-risk environments. Ideally, in circumstances such as Haiti's, new, high-risk investment programs would offer not only insurance (which OPIC does very well) but also working capital loans at concessional rates—despite the enhanced credit risks. Establishing international capabilities to encourage such activity would also be valuable—although, again, the United States gains more leverage with every tool that it controls.

Economic growth—even over the short term—is impossible in Haiti without private investment from abroad. In fact, in Haiti foreign investors were almost wholly responsible for the growth and subsequent contraction of the assembly sector, the primary non-agricultural employer in a job-starved economy. Many of these investors were American. (This is not to say that Haitians do not need to invest in their own country. Investment by local business people is key. However, the ability of Haitians to invest in amounts large enough to make a visible difference was and is nonexistent.)

In many reconstruction or peacekeeping initiatives, the creation of jobs was among the most important near-term stabilizers and signs that the "new order" was producing positive results. The U.S. government had limited resources to support the creation of 50-60 thousand short-term, public works–type jobs in Haiti. The World Bank later picked up important portions of this program, but everyone involved knew that even these aid-supported minimum-wage jobs would not last. Consequently, the U.S. government had strong reasons to want to induce U.S. companies to return to Haiti.

Unfortunately, in a high-risk environment, the only way to induce such a return is to mitigate risk and provide working capital to the would-be returnees—many of whom in Haiti's case had been badly hurt by the embargo that preceded Aristide's return. U.S. programs to do this proved ill-suited to the task, because they were not really conceived with this particular kind of task in mind. Furthermore, the lack of banking infrastructure in Haiti severely limited the options for the implementation of such a program.

In the Middle East, OPIC had the responsibility for disbursing $125 million to attract businesses into the Territories. OPIC chairwoman Ruth Harkin led missions to the region and repeatedly reiterated the high priority that the agency would give to development in the Territories. But virtually no deals were made. There were several reasons for this. One is that business people were repeatedly scared away by events in the region. Another is that some of the projects that were placed before OPIC, and even urged on OPIC, were bad business deals. Yet another reason involved OPIC's avoidance of any sensitive projects as a consequence of the agency's precarious political situation.

However, the overriding reason why OPIC was unproductive in the Palestinian Territories is the same as why it was unproductive in Haiti. OPIC was created to foster investment on commercial terms. It is the wrong tool to foster high-risk investments in volatile environments such as the Middle East and Haiti, yet such situations are precisely where the right tools are badly needed. (That said, one cannot help speculating about how OPIC developed such an extensive portfolio in Russia.)

In Bosnia, the responsibility for stimulating economic growth lay with several agencies in addition to AID, including OPIC, the Trade and Development Agency (TDA), and the Department of Commerce. All made high-profile inroads for their Bosnia program. TDA, which funds feasibility studies for major projects and plays a vital role in getting the infrastructure ball rolling, was much more active in Bosnia than in either Haiti or the Middle East, and the benefits for Bosnia and U.S. companies were clearer thanks to Bosnia's proximity to the prosperous markets of Western Europe and the transitional markets of Central and Eastern Europe. TDA worked through a list of hundreds of projects to winnow it down to the 40 or 50 that could actually get done and that offered a role for U.S. companies.

Meanwhile, OPIC had learned a substantial lesson about the dangers of inflated expectations from its Haiti and Middle East experiences. When Ruth Harkin went to Bosnia and signed an agreement enabling OPIC to provide much-needed insurance to help attract private sector businesses to the region, she sensibly did not cite a specific amount of assistance that would be offered, so that a failure to hit that number would not be a letdown.

U.S. interests would be best served, however, by special programs that can attract the private sector to high-risk situations and that can hit the disbursement targets necessary for achieving our foreign policy goals.

The effort of the Commerce Department to actually bring businesses to Bosnia was marred by the tragic death of Commerce Secretary Ron Brown and thirty-four others. Later, Brown's successor, Mickey Kantor, made this trip with another group of business people. However, both trips were primarily symbolic, deepening the tragedy further. Symbolism does have a role, and the commitment of those who died to advance the cause of peace cannot be questioned. Former Assistant Secretary Holbrooke is on the record saying he urged the Brown trip because he felt that reconstruction was so important to ultimate peace. He was correct. But the private sector is not a magic bullet that can fill the void left by low official giving; nor will businesses invest in high-risk environments for the sake of serving U.S. foreign policy objectives.

Ron Brown went to Bosnia without the real tools needed to make deals happen. Those tools are financial and must be specially designed to fund projects in high-risk venues.

EPILOGUE: THE FUTURE OF EMERGENCY ECONOMIC INTERVENTION

During the two years in which the work on this book was done, much has changed. Optimism about the Middle East peace process has been undercut by repeated shocks. Terrorist attacks, political upheaval, altered positions, intransigence, and the politically and economically decaying atmosphere in the region at large have all taken their toll. In Bosnia, political setbacks, grassroots resistance to the reintegration of society, and the rise of new nationalist voices have led to a sense that the prospects of future political or military crises overshadow the gradual efforts to rebuild what war destroyed. In Haiti, the increasingly overt resistance of former President Aristide and his supporters to the reforms he once promised to lead has caused the nation to spend the latter half of 1997 without a Prime Minister or a functioning government. A sense of hopelessness has returned to the people of that benighted country, and the window of opportunity opened by Aristide's return effectively has shut for now.

Despite this discouraging record, several other facts have become clear. First, the emergency economic interventions in these countries did relieve suffering, build good will, and improve the chances of peace, though they subsequently faltered. Second, had these efforts been more successful, the chances for peace or at least prolonged stability would have improved. Third, the volatility of each of these situations suggests that U.S. policy-makers will have to intervene economically again. Finally, and perhaps most important, other potential crises are on the horizon that will certainly demand that our political and military efforts be complemented by effective economic initiatives—initiatives that the American people and our leaders have every right to expect to be more effective than those undertaken during the first term of the Clinton Administration.

TRANSITION IN NORTH KOREA

One situation in which the economic dimensions of crisis resolution will certainly be of great concern to the United States is that in North Korea. For several years it has been apparent that the isolated, poverty-stricken police state on the northern half of the Korean peninsula is unstable and cannot survive in its current incarnation. Since the death of Kim Il Sung and the succession of his son Kim Jong Il, the situation has deteriorated. Today, North Korea is an economic disaster;

there are reports of widespread starvation and crushing deprivation at every level of society. At the same time, North Korea remains a rogue state, heavily armed and a threat to U.S. interests in Asia and, through its cooperation with other rogue states, elsewhere in the world.

North Korea may react or succumb to its crisis in a variety of ways: One is war. While war is increasingly less likely, given the dwindling resources of the nation, the state's posture is still belligerent. Some see the North's leadership initiating a conflict with the South as a possible desperation move. Even in the likely event of Pyongyang's defeat, its leadership might view this scenario as the one by which they might have the greatest influence over their destiny. A more likely course would be for the leadership, pressured by its current economic straits, to negotiate a peace treaty with the South that calls for reopening its borders and seeks aid in rebuilding. While quadripartite discussions between Pyongyang and Seoul—and including the United States and China—have recently gotten off to a productive start in Geneva, it should be remembered that North and South have lived side by side for over four decades without such a treaty, and hostility still runs high. Indeed, many South Korean leaders have advocated that North Korea simply be squeezed so hard through further isolation from the world economy that it ultimately collapses and awaits the disposition of the South.

In contemplation of this last scenario and variants of it, South Korea's government and business leaders have invited into the country a steady stream of economists, including many who worked on the reunification of Germany. Although estimates for the cost of rebuilding North Korea vary from $200 billion over ten years to over a trillion dollars over an undefined period, there is a consensus on the difficulty with which the reconstruction will be achieved. Germany has seen over $600 billion flowing from West to East in the seven years since reunification—just 5 percent of output. For South Korea however, the burden may be much greater; the estimates above would amount to 8 percent of output at the very least. Furthermore, the South Koreans are faced with improving the standard of living of a population half their size, whereas East Germany's population was only a quarter that of West Germany. North Korea's income per capita is one-tenth that of South Korea, whereas East Germany's income per capita was already one-third of West Germany's. Some in the South have advocated that this process of transition and reconstruction proceed slowly. *Chaebol* leaders have in fact fantasized aloud about turning the North into a low-wage export platform for South Korean companies. On the one hand, this may be the most affordable approach to the problem. On the other, it is likely to produce great resentment in the North.

The situation has been made much more complex by the recent

financial collapse in South Korea and elsewhere in Asia. Almost all scenarios for smooth transition to either a more open, restructured North or to a unified Korea were developed with the assumption that South Korea would be economically strong. Today, the country is in the throes of the greatest economic crisis in its history and seems almost certainly to be on the verge of a recession—or worse—that could last three to five years. Unfortunately, this is precisely the period during which the North's transition to one new existence or another is likely to take place. Therefore, the natural engine of growth by which North Korea could be pulled out of its economic depths is going to be weaker. If unemployment rises in the South, which is likely, creating programs that employ lower-wage Northerners will be unpopular. Furthermore, in any eventuality, the political strength of the South Korean government will be compromised for some time to come.

The financial crisis also means that the international community will be forced to play a very large role in facilitating any transition on the peninsula at a time when its own ability to do so will be compromised. The cost of bailouts in Asia, and the possible need for future bailouts of Russia, Brazil, and other countries, places a heavy burden on international institutions and the contributors to those institutions. The consequences of the economic crisis in the region are likely to be global and to result in recession in Southeast Asia, Japan, and South Korea; continuing sluggishness in Europe; and depressed rates of growth in the United States—and thus to constrain the ability or willingness of potential donors to act. This threat to the will needed to cushion a transition on the Korean peninsula will be exacerbated by the growing tendency of the U.S. Congress toward isolationism and its micro-management of global initiatives. Furthermore, as is the case in Bosnia, the international community is divided over the kind of Korea that it wants to emerge. Japan certainly does not want to see a united Korea. China does not want to see a significantly strengthened Korea—nor, for that matter, may Russia. Meanwhile, reunification and/or significant North-South economic ties offer certain advantages to the United States, which seeks to balance other powers in the region and has a long-standing, close relationship with the government of the Republic of Korea. The government in the North, or of a reunified Korea, is of course likely to have certain philosophical differences with the United States and other donors related either to past ideologies (be they communist or statist) or to new ambitions.

Thus, in Korea, we are likely to face a situation of the highest sensitivity in which many of the challenges will be similar to those in the cases discussed in this book. The stakes will be high, and unless we apply lessons learned, our Korea efforts are likely to suffer the same shortcomings as those experienced in Haiti, the Middle East, and Bosnia. That is a price we can ill afford to pay.

CUBA AFTER CASTRO

It is also likely that during the next several years Fidel Castro will leave office. The various succession scenarios all suggest that the United States must be prepared to intervene economically in Cuba in order to promote an outcome that is consistent with U.S. policy toward the island country.

In one scenario, Castro will be succeeded by his brother or another leader from the Cuban communist establishment. Most observers feel that any such leader is likely to be considerably weaker than Fidel. While this could produce a temporary tightening of the government's control over society, it is unlikely to be sustainable given the country's economic plight and the weakness of the government. Such conditions could quite possibly lead to the introduction of reforms or diplomatic initiatives designed to stimulate the flow of international investment into Cuba.

Should the new leadership appear to be vulnerable, or in the event that a communist succession cannot be managed by the leadership, Cuba may face a political crisis. The active, well-financed Cuban community in Miami might try to prompt and/or support an insurgency against the communist government. Whether this leads to a military confrontation or simply to a new government, Cuba would find itself at an economic and political crossroads.

The country has suffered greatly since the fall of the Soviet Union. As a result of the collapse of export partners in the Soviet bloc and the elimination of aid from the U.S.S.R., Cuban GDP has fallen substantially since 1991. According to independent analysts, tightening of the U.S. embargo pursuant to the Helms-Burton Act has produced a measurable decline in investment in Cuba—this despite the fact that, of all the countries in this Hemisphere, only the United States is seeking to isolate the Castro regime.

When the current Cuban government is forced to adopt a new political and economic approach, or when there is a new government, the United States—which has taken a unique and resolute stance in refusing to normalize relations until major reforms are under way—will find itself under heavy pressure to ensure the reformists' success and to put Cuba in our "good neighbor" column for keeps. This pressure will emanate from the active Cuban communities in Florida and New Jersey, among others, which have been expert at influencing U.S. policy-making and which would have the greatest stake in seeing a re-opened Cuba prosper.

There is a low likelihood, however, that the desires of the Cuban people will match identically the desires of the Cuban-American population that drives much of U.S. policy. In any event, Washington's policy response to political change in Cuba will certainly include a major economic initiative that will require the support of decision-makers who understand the core issues raised in this book. Much Cuban reconstruction can be private-sector driven—assuming the transition to a new regime is smooth and does not create disincentives to private sector involvement. A special challenge and irony will be that, should Cuba undergo a transition in the fairly near future, then rebuilding Cuba—and in particular attempting to attract industry and investment to Cuba—is likely to create distracting new competition for the programs that may still be in place in Haiti, only a few minutes distant by plane.

But the primary point regarding Cuba is this: For thirty years, engineering the fall of the Castro regime has been a prime U.S. foreign policy objective. Now, with the realization of that objective in sight one way or another, and with the consequences of that fall clear to all who even casually consider the issue, the United States has done little to prepare contingency plans for consolidating the nearing long-sought triumph over Cuban communism. We even know a number of the key issues that policy-makers will have to consider, including: the resolution of expropriation cases in order to get U.S. funds flowing; helping replace outdated infrastructure (a prerequisite for private sector investment flows and stabilization); addressing the inadequacies of Cuban commercial legislation (our experience in transitional economies in Eastern and Central Europe should be helpful here); and dealing with our sugar quota and concerns, particularly from neighboring Florida, about competing imports, especially those from the agricultural sector. The handwriting is on the wall. What is the U.S. government going to do about it?

OTHER CRISES—FROM THE GULF TO THE FORMER SOVIET UNION TO AFRICA

Many other hot spots in the world could quickly produce unrest and the demand for a peacekeeping effort that includes—indeed, depends on—economic reconstruction and economic transition initiatives. Potential crisis situations that would require international intervention include: another conflict either in the Gulf or between Israel and its neighbors; a succession struggle in Saudi Arabia reflecting divisions between fundamentalists and moderates in that society; further attempts to de-stabilize Egypt; escalated conflict between Turkey and Kurdistan; the spread of conflict from the Balkans into Kosovo, Macedonia, and beyond; Russia and other independent states that have emerged from the former Soviet Union; continuing turmoil in Congo and Central Africa; the rekindling of traditional hostilities in India and Pakistan; renewed fighting in Northern Ireland; and even the potential for trouble in Mexico following, for example, political conflict in outlying provinces, perhaps sparked by fighting between drug lords and the federal government.

In each case, a premium would be placed on reducing military risk and ensuring sustainable peace. Consequently, the same rationales and constraints that governed U.S. interventions in Haiti, the Middle East, and Bosnia would govern our efforts and those of our allies in each of these regions.

I therefore conclude this book even more certain than I was when we began this study that the issues addressed here are of considerable and enduring importance and warrant the careful study and deliberate action of the U.S. government. The steps that have been taken to date remain inadequate at best—despite the earnest, honorable motivations behind most of them. I hope that this book will prompt policy-makers to give greater consideration to the exigencies of emergency economics. If they do not, the price of peace will be needlessly high in the future.

ABOUT THE AUTHOR

David J. Rothkopf is co-founder and President of the Newmarket Company LLC., a Washington D.C.–based provider of international information and advisory services specializing in the world's emerging markets. He is also an Adjunct Professor of International Affairs at Columbia University's School of International and Public Affairs and at the Georgetown School of Foreign Service. Prior to establishing Newmarket in January 1998, Mr. Rothkopf was Managing Director and Member of the Board of Kissinger Associates, Inc.

Mr. Rothkopf earlier served as Acting Under Secretary of Commerce for International Trade, in which capacity he led Commerce's International Trade Administration; and as Deputy Under Secretary of Commerce for International Trade Policy Development, leading and developing the Clinton Administration's Big Emerging Markets Initiative. While at Commerce, Mr. Rothkopf had responsibility for all aspects of trade policy for the Department, chaired the Department's Asia and Latin America task forces, and oversaw the development of the Administration's aggressive advocacy efforts on behalf of U.S. companies in major projects worldwide. From November 1994 to January 1996, Mr. Rothkopf also served as coordinator of the U.S. government's economic recovery initiative for Haiti.

Prior to joining the government, Mr. Rothkopf held a variety of senior positions in the private sector dealing with international trade issues, including service as Chairman and Chief Executive Officer of International Media Partners. At IMP, he was editor-in-chief and publisher of IMP publications, including *CEO/International Strategies* magazine, and of IMP's CEO Institutes, one of the world's leading organizers of international affairs conferences and seminars for top business executives.

Mr. Rothkopf has written extensively—for a wide variety of journals, magazines, and newspapers worldwide—on a broad array of international trade, economic, and political issues. He is co-author of a textbook on the Common Market, published in 1978, and served as principal author of *The Big Emerging Markets* (Bernan Press, 1995). He is also a co-author of *U.S. Commercial Diplomacy* (Council on Foreign Relations, 1998).

Mr. Rothkopf holds a B.A. from Columbia College of Columbia University and attended the Columbia University Graduate School of Journalism.

MEMBERS OF THE STUDY GROUP

Morton I. Abramowitz is a Senior Fellow at the Council on Foreign Relations in their Washington, D.C. office. He served as President of the Carnegie Endowment for International Peace from 1991 to 1997. Prior to joining the Endowment, he was Ambassador to Turkey. Mr. Abramowitz also served as Assistant Secretary of State for Intelligence and Research; as U.S. Ambassador to the Mutual and Balanced Force Reduction Negotiations in Vienna; as Ambassador to Thailand; and as Deputy Assistant Secretary of Defense for Inter-American, East Asian and Pacific Affairs. He is the author (with Richard Moorsteen) of *Remaking China Policy* (1972), *Moving the Glacier: The Two Koreas and the Powers* (1972), and *China: Can We Have a Policy?* (1996). He has published numerous articles and essays on subjects ranging from U.S. foreign policy to issues relating to the former Yugoslavia.

Nicole Ball is a Fellow at the Overseas Development Council (ODC), which fosters understanding of how development relates to a much-changed U.S. domestic and international policy agenda. In 1992-94, she directed the ODC Program on Security and Development, which examined how the international development community can assist countries in moving from war to peace. Ms. Ball has also acted as a consultant on numerous subjects relating to the war-to-peace transition. Since 1978, Ms. Ball's many publications on the relationship between military security and development in the developing world include the policy essay, *Making Peace Work: The Role of the International Development Community*. Her other publications include *Pressing for Peace: Can Aid Induce Reform* (1992) and *Demobilization and Reintegration of Military Personnel in Africa* (1993).

Amy S. Borrus is a correspondent for *Business Week*, and she has covered U.S. trade and foreign policy from the magazine's Washington bureau for six years. Prior to that, she was a correspondent in the magazine's Tokyo and London bureaus and was briefly a regional reporter for *Business Week* in the United States. In 1992, she received an Overseas Press Club award for a series of stories about China.

Thomas Carothers is Director of Research at the Carnegie Endowment for International Peace in Washington, D.C., and co-director of its Democracy Project. He first joined the Endowment as a Senior Associate working on issues relating to the promotion of democracy abroad. He has worked on democracy assistance projects in Asia, Eastern Europe, the former Soviet Union, Latin America, and Africa. He has also written extensively on the subject, including two books, *Assessing Democracy Assistance: The Case of Romania* (1996) and *In the Name of Democracy: U.S. Policy Toward Latin America in the Reagan Years* (1991), as well as numerous articles. Prior to joining the Carnegie Endowment, Mr. Carothers practiced international and corporate law at the law firm of Arnold & Porter in Washington, D.C., and worked in the Office of the Legal Adviser of the U.S. Department of

State. He has been an International Affairs Fellow of the Council on Foreign Relations, a Guest Scholar at the Woodrow Wilson International Center for Scholars, and a Visiting Scholar at the School of Advanced International Studies (SAIS) of Johns Hopkins University.

Richard A. Clarke is Special Assistant to the President for National Security Affairs and Senior Director of Global Issues on the staff of the National Security Council—positions he has held since the beginning of the first Clinton Administration. Mr. Clarke is a career officer of the U.S. government's Senior Executive Service. In the Bush Administration, he served as Assistant Secretary of State for Politico-Military Affairs. During the Reagan Administration, he was Deputy Assistant Secretary of State for Intelligence. Prior to these appointments, he held positions in the Defense Department and the State Department, beginning in 1973.

Amy Kaslow is an independent journalist reporting on international economic developments. Since May, 1996, Ms. Kaslow has been a Senior Fellow in Economics and Employment at the Council on Competitiveness in Washington, D.C. From 1989 to 1996, she was the chief economic correspondent for the *Christian Science Monitor*, covering a wide array of issues related to money. Under the auspices of the Washington-based Center for Strategic and International Studies (CSIS), she co-authored a study on international labor issues for the 1994 Group of Seven Jobs Summit in Detroit. She has published features and opinion pieces in numerous newspapers and journals, and as an editorial board member has been a regular contributor to both *Europe Magazine* and *Middle East Insight*.

Susan Levine joined the Emerging Markets Partnership in 1997, as the Principal Adviser to the AIG Asian Infrastructure Fund, after serving for nearly four years in the Clinton Administration. Ms. Levine joined the Overseas Private Investment Corporation in 1995 as Senior Vice President for Policy and Investment Development, and she directed the agency's business development efforts in places such as West Bank/Gaza, Haiti, Central Asia, and Cambodia. In 1993-95, Ms. Levine was Deputy Assistant Secretary of the Treasury for International Development, Debt and Environmental Policy. Her responsibilities included U.S. participation in the multilateral development banks. Prior to joining the U.S. Treasury Department, Ms. Levine was a Senior Vice President at Lehman Brothers, where she ran the Private Equity Placement Group. She was responsible for structuring and placing transactions for both private and public companies in a wide variety of sectors, including telecommunications and media.

Moisés Naím is the Editor of *Foreign Policy* magazine. From 1992 to 1996, he was a Senior Associate and director of Latin America programs at the Carnegie Endowment for International Peace. During 1996, he also served as a Senior Advisor to the President of the World Bank. He has written extensively on economic development, the politics and economics of international trade and investment, and the causes and consequences of global integration. He is the author or editor of five books, has published numerous academic articles, and writes frequently for newspapers and magazines in the United States, Europe, and Latin America. Dr. Naím served as Venezuela's Minister of Trade and Industry and played a central role in that government's 1989 launching of major economic reforms. Prior to his ministerial position, he served as the Dean of IESA, one of South America's leading business schools and research centers. In 1995, the *Washington Post* identified Moisés Naím as one of Latin America's fifteen most influential young leaders.

Ernest H. Preeg has held the William M. Scholl Chair in International Business at the Center for Strategic and International Studies since 1988. Before joining CSIS, he served as chief economist at the U.S. Agency for International Development beginning in 1986. A career foreign service officer, Dr. Preeg served as U.S. Ambassador to Haiti from 1981 to 1983. Prior to that, Dr. Preeg was executive director of the White House Economic Policy Group, Deputy Assistant Secretary of State for International Finance and Development, and Director of the Office of European Communities and OECD Affairs. His numerous books include *The Haitian Dilemma* (1996), *Cuba and the New Caribbean Economic Order* (1993), and *Traders in a Brave New World* (1995).

William D. Rogers is a senior partner in the Washington law firm of Arnold & Porter. He concentrates on international financial and monetary matters, on international public law issues for several governments and international organizations, and on international arbitration. In 1974-77, Mr. Rogers served in the U.S. State Department, first as Assistant Secretary of State for Inter-American Affairs and later as Under Secretary of State for Economic Affairs. After his return to Arnold & Porter, he remained active in international affairs, serving in several capacities, including special emissary of President Carter to El Salvador in 1980, co-chairman of the Bilateral Commission on the Future of U.S.–Mexican Relations, and Senior Counselor to the National Bipartisan Commission on Central America. Mr. Rogers has served as President of the American Society of International Law and is a three-term member of the Board of Directors of the Council on Foreign Relations in New York. He is a Vice Chairman of Kissinger Associates Inc. and is the author of various publications on foreign relations.

Stanley O. Roth is currently serving as Assistant Secretary for East Asian and Pacific Affairs at the U.S. Department of State. In 1996-97, he was Director of Research and Studies at the U.S. Institute of Peace. While at the Institute, he was asked to serve as a Clinton Administration envoy to six Asian countries concerning Burma. Prior to joining the Institute, Mr. Roth was Special Assistant to the President and Senior Director for Asian Affairs at the National Security Council; Deputy Assistant Secretary of Defense for East Asian and Pacific Affairs; and Director of Committee Liaison for the United States House of Representative Committee on Foreign Affairs. In 1985-92, Mr. Roth was Staff Director to the Subcommittee on Asian and Pacific Affairs of the House Foreign Affairs Committee, conducting more than 150 hearings on all aspects of U.S.–Asia policy and traveling extensively to almost every country in the region with various Congressional delegations.

James A. Schear is Deputy Assistant Secretary of Defense for Peacekeeping and Humanitarian Assistance, a position he has held since 1997. He was previously a Resident Associate at the Carnegie Endowment for International Peace, where he focused on the roles and limitations of international peacekeeping operations in post-conflict transitions. Prior to joining the Endowment, Dr. Schear was a Senior Associate at the Henry L. Stimson Center. During 1992-95, he served as a policy consultant to the United Nations, performing field assessments of U.N. civilian and military operations in Cambodia and the former Yugoslavia. In the 1980s, Dr. Schear held research appointments at the International Institute for Strategic Studies, Harvard University's Center for Science and International Affairs, and the Brookings Institution. He has edited three books and contributed chapters and articles to many books, journals, and newspapers.

PARTICIPANTS IN ROUNDTABLE DISCUSSIONS

BOSNIA ROUNDTABLE

Ambassador Sven Alkalaj
*Embassy of the Republic of
Bosnia and Herzegovina to
the United States*

Kemal Dervis
World Bank

Thomas Dine
*U.S. Agency for
International Development*

Nancy Ely-Raphel
U.S. Department of State

John Fox
Open Society Institute

Zdenka Gast
*Contractors Welding of
Western New York, Inc.*

Marshall Harris
Balkan Institute

James Holmes
U.S. Department of State

Michael Marek
World Bank

Sherwood McGinnis
U.S. Department of State

Richard Murphy
Council on Foreign Relations

Nenad Porges
*Embassy of Croatia to
the United States*

Ambassador Muhamed Sacirbey
*Permanent Mission of the Republic of
Bosnia and Herzegovina to the U.N.*

Alexander Vershbow
National Security Council

Christine Wallich
World Bank

Warren Zimmerman
Columbia University

HAITI ROUNDTABLE

Walter Bastian
U.S. Department of Commerce

Robert Burke
*U.S. Agency for
International Development*

Ambassador Jean Casimir
*Embassy of Haiti to the
United States*

Lauri Fitz-Pegado
U.S. Department of Commerce

Michael Sheehan
National Security Council

Leslie Voltaire
Presidential Palace, Haiti

MIDDLE EAST ROUNDTABLE

Colette Avatel
Israeli Consulate, New York

Rex Brynen
McGill University

Jan Kalicki
U.S. Department of Commerce

Ambassador Itamar Rabinovich
*Embassy of Israel to the
United States*

Hasan Rahman
Palestine Affairs Center

John Robinson, Jr.
Black & Veatch

Toni Verstandig
U.S. Department of State

THE CARNEGIE ENDOWMENT FOR INTERNATIONAL PEACE

The Carnegie Endowment for International Peace was established in 1910 in Washington, D.C., with a gift from Andrew Carnegie. As a tax-exempt operating (not grant-making) foundation, the Endowment conducts programs of research, discussion, publication, and education in international affairs and U.S. foreign policy. The Endowment publishes the quarterly magazine, *Foreign Policy*.

Carnegie's senior associates—whose backgrounds include government, journalism, law, academia, and public affairs—bring to their work substantial first-hand experience in foreign policy. Through writing, public and media appearances, study groups, and conferences, Carnegie associates seek to invigorate and extend both expert and public discussion on a wide range of international issues, including worldwide migration, nuclear non-proliferation, regional conflicts, multilateralism, democracy building, and the use of force. The Endowment also engages in and encourages projects designed to foster innovative contributions in international affairs.

In 1993, the Carnegie Endowment committed its resources to the establishment of a public policy research center in Moscow designed to promote intellectual collaboration among scholars and specialists in the United States, Russia, and other post-Soviet states. Together with the Endowment's associates in Washington, the center's staff of Russian and American specialists conduct programs on a broad range of major policy issues ranging from economic reform to civil-military relations. The Carnegie Moscow Center holds seminars, workshops, and study groups at which international participants from academia, government, journalism, the private sector, and non-governmental institutions gather to exchange views. It also provides a forum for prominent international figures to present their views to informed Moscow audiences. Associates of the center also host seminars in Kiev on an equally broad set of topics.

The Endowment normally does not take institutional positions on public policy issues. It supports its activities primarily from its own resources, supplemented by non-governmental, philanthropic grants.

Carnegie Endowment for International Peace
1779 Massachusetts Ave., N.W.
Washington, D.C. 20036
Tel: 202-483-7600
Fax: 202-483-1840
e-mail: carnegie@ceip.org
Web Page: www.ceip.org

Carnegie Moscow Center
Ul. Tverskaya 16/2
7th Floor
Moscow 103009
Tel: 7-095-935-8904
Fax: 7-095- 935-8906
e-mail: info@carnegie.ru
Web Page: www.carnegie.ru

102

A CARNEGIE ENDOWMENT BOOK
POINT OF NO RETURN
THE DEADLY STRUGGLE FOR MIDDLE EAST PEACE

GEOFFREY KEMP AND JEREMY PRESSMAN

The Arab-Israeli peace process has passed a point of no return. Yet there is no guarantee of further peace treaties between Israel, the Arab states, and the Palestinians. A comprehensive Middle East settlement including Iran and Turkey is even less certain. The authors argue that three fundamental preconditions are necessary for regional peace: a continuing and assertive U.S. role; a final Israeli-Palestinian settlement; and continued structural economic reform by the key regional players. If the region's countries by default or preference continue to put off tough choices and to perpetrate the hatreds of the past, they will have no one to blame but themselves for the inevitable disasters that will follow.

Geoffrey Kemp, formerly Director of the Carnegie Endowment's Middle East Arms Control Project, is Director of Regional Strategic Programs at the Nixon Center for Peace and Freedom. **Jeremy Pressman** is a former Carnegie Endowment Project Associate.

"Point of No Return is an extraordinary achievement. It describes and dissects the Middle East conflict both in its whole and in its parts—with complete realism and rare balance. No other work so well succeeds in both getting to the heart of all the issues in Arab-Israeli peacemaking and describing the other conflicts which torment the region and which so condition the outlook for truly comprehensive peace. This book is an authentic *tour de force."*
—**Samuel W. Lewis,** U.S. Ambassador to Israel, 1977-85

"A most timely book but one that has lasting value for understanding the much talked about but little understood Middle East peace process and the environment that shapes it."
—**Mohammed Wahby,** Columnist, *Al-Mussawar* (Cairo)

"A valuable survey of the current Middle East and Gulf environment in the context of the search for peace. Its importance lies in summing up the significant advances in the Arab-Israeli peace process and relating them to the larger Middle East/Gulf situation."
—**Roscoe S. Suddarth,** President, Middle East Institute

"Tells the reader almost everything he/she needs to know about the quest for peace in the Middle East and the forces pressing for and against the continuation of the peace process."
—**Shai Feldman,** Head, Jaffee Center for Strategic Studies, Tel Aviv University

$18.95 in paper (ISBN 0-87003-021-3); $44.95 in cloth (ISBN 0-87003-020-5)

To order, please call Carnegie's distributor, Brookings Institution Press, 1-800-275-1447 (toll-free in the United States) or 202-797-6258. Fax: 202-797-6004. Address: Brookings Institution Press, Dept. 029, Washington, D.C. 20042-0029.

A CARNEGIE/ASPEN BOOK
UNFINISHED PEACE
REPORT OF THE INTERNATIONAL COMMISSION ON THE BALKANS

"Superb report"—*Newsweek International*

The guns have fallen silent in the former Yugoslavia. But the Dayton truce has yet to become a lasting peace. Peace in the Balkans remains threatened not only by the possibility of a new war in Bosnia, but also by unresolved conflict in Kosovo and Macedonia.

At the end of the twentieth century, as at its beginning, the Balkans stand at a crossroads, facing the choice of being marginalized, or overcoming their problems

and creating the conditions for their integration into the European mainstream. The stakes for the West are also high. Another war in the region might not threaten the West directly, but it would have a corrosive effect on Western unity. Stopping a new conflagration would require a large-scale Western intervention; another failure to intervene would raise more questions about what values the Western democracies are willing to defend.

The International Commission on the Balkans was established in July 1995 by the Aspen Institute Berlin and the Carnegie Endowment for International Peace to provide an independent perspective on the region's continuing problems and to propose a concerted Western approach to long-term stability.

Drawing on its extensive, high-level, and politically comprehensive discussions throughout the region, the Commission examines the causes of the recent Balkan conflicts and provides an independent assessment of the European, American, and U.N. responses to them. It calls for a wide range of stabilizing measures—including proposals for the treatment of minorities, the promotion of democracy, and Balkan cooperation. To be effective, the Commission warns, such efforts must be reinforced by NATO's continuing and coherent military engagement.

MEMBERS OF THE COMMISSION: Leo Tindemans, Chairman; Lloyd Cutler, Bronislaw Geremek, John Roper, Theo Sommer, Simone Veil, and David Anderson (ex officio).

224 pp. ISBN: 0-87003-118-X   Price: $14.95

To order, please call Carnegie's distributor, Brookings Institution Press,
1-800-275-1447 (toll-free in the United States) or 202-797-6258. Fax: 202-797-6004.
Address: Brookings Institution Press, Dept. 029, Washington, D.C. 20042-0029.